Eyewitness
MESOPOTAMIA

Mesopotamian account tablet in cuneiform
script, c. 2050 BCE

Spinning with a drop spindle, a
tool used in Sumer before 2000 BCE

Leaf and
fruits of the
date palm, native
to the Fertile Crescent

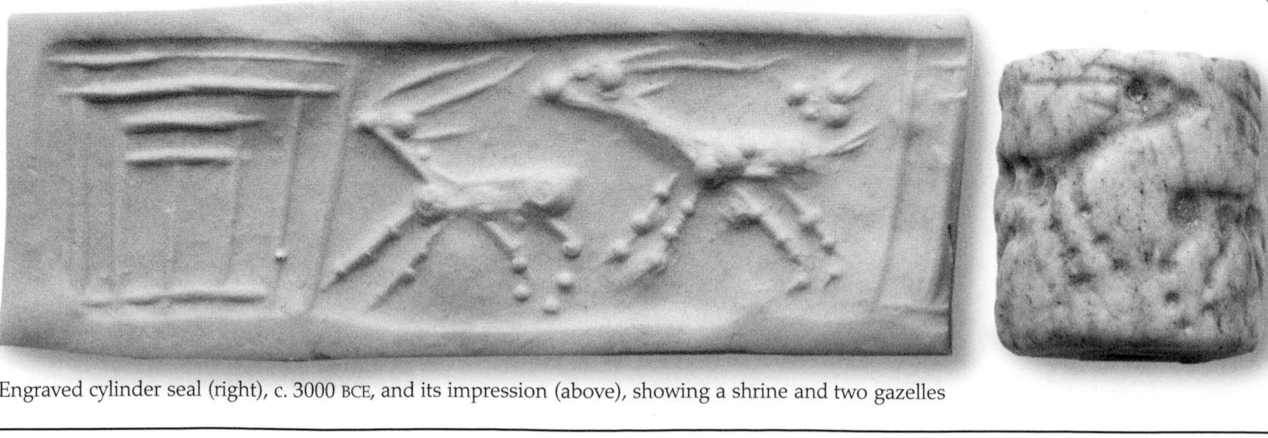

Engraved cylinder seal (right), c. 3000 BCE, and its impression (above), showing a shrine and two gazelles

Pear, a fruit grown in Mesopotamia's irrigated gardens

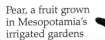

Thyme, used by Babylonian physicians as an antiseptic

Eyewitness
MESOPOTAMIA

Written by
PHILIP STEELE

Model planked wheel, the same design used for early Mesopotamian wheels, c. 3200 BCE

DK Publishing, Inc.

Wheat, first farmed
in Mesopotamia
before 9500 BCE

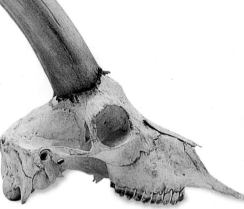

Skull of a wild goat, an animal domesticated in
Mesopotamia c. 8000 BCE

LONDON, NEW YORK,
MELBOURNE, MUNICH, AND DELHI

Consultant Dr. Eleanor Robson

Project editor Clare Hibbert
Art editor Neville Graham
Senior art editor David Ball
Managing editor Camilla Hallinan
Managing art editor Martin Wilson
Publishing manager Sunita Gahir
Category publisher Andrea Pinnington
Picture research Claire Bowers, Sarah Hopper, Rose Horridge
Production controller Angela Graef
Jacket designer Neal Cobourne
Jacket editor Adam Powley

DK DELHI:

Head of publishing Aparna Sharma
Senior designer Romi Chakraborty
DTP designer Govind Mittal

First published in the United States in 2007 by
DK Publishing
375 Hudson Street
New York, New York 10014

A catalog record for this book is available from the Library of Congress.

ISBN: 978-0-7566-2972-4 (HC) 978-0-7566-2971-7 (Library Binding)

Color reproduction by Colourscan, Singapore
Printed and bound by Toppan Printing Co., (Shenzhen) Ltd., China

Dates in this book are given as BCE (Before Common Era,
comparable to years BC or Before Christ) and CE (Common Era,
comparable to years after AD or *Anno Domini*)

Discover more at
www.dk.com

Raw lapis lazuli

Silver drinking horn from
Susa, fifth century BCE

Pomegranate and pistachio nuts,
fruits of Mesopotamian gardens

A trowel, hand pick, and brush,
all tools of the archeologist

An Assyrian king in his hunting chariot

Contents

Assyrian necklace of gold, lapis lazuli, carnelian, quartz, and malachite, c. 1300 BCE

Land between two rivers

TWO GREAT RIVERS FLOW SOUTHWARD through the Middle East. The region between them is sometimes called the cradle of civilization. It was here, from around 3500 BCE, that the first cities, states, and empires arose. The people who lived there did not have a name for the whole region, but the ancient Greeks called it Mesopotamia, meaning "between the rivers." Home to the Sumerian, Assyrian, and Babylonian civilizations, Mesopotamia was the birthplace of writing, as well as many other inventions and discoveries that changed the world.

TIGRIS RIVER
The easternmost of the Middle East's two great rivers is the Tigris, which rises in the Taurus Mountains of Turkey. It joins up with its twin, the Euphrates, near Al-Qurna in Iraq. Together they flow south into the Gulf. Ancient Mesopotamia depended on these rivers for water.

WHERE WAS MESOPOTAMIA?
Most of ancient Mesopotamia lay within the borders of modern Iraq. At times it also extended into parts of what are now Turkey, Syria, and southwestern Iran. Much of the region is now hot desert, but many areas were much more fertile in antiquity. Mesopotamia also included cooler mountainous regions in the north and reed-filled wetlands in the southeast.

Female figure made of terra-cotta

PREHISTORIC POTTERY
This clay figure was made in a style named after the Tell (or mound) of Halaf, an archeological site in northern Syria. The figure is about 7,000 years old and was an offering to the gods. The Halaf people built some of Mesopotamia's earliest villages. They raised cattle, sheep, and goats, and grew barley, wheat, and flax. They also produced distinctive pottery, painted in black, white, and red.

WHERE HISTORY BEGAN
A sacred monument called a ziggurat rises from the ancient site of Ur, in southern Iraq. Ur was a powerful, wealthy city as early as 2500 BCE. The great age of the Mesopotamian civilizations and empires lasted from around 3000 BCE until 539 BCE. This period is sometimes seen as the beginning of history, because during this time people began to write down historical records of their battles and peace treaties and laws.

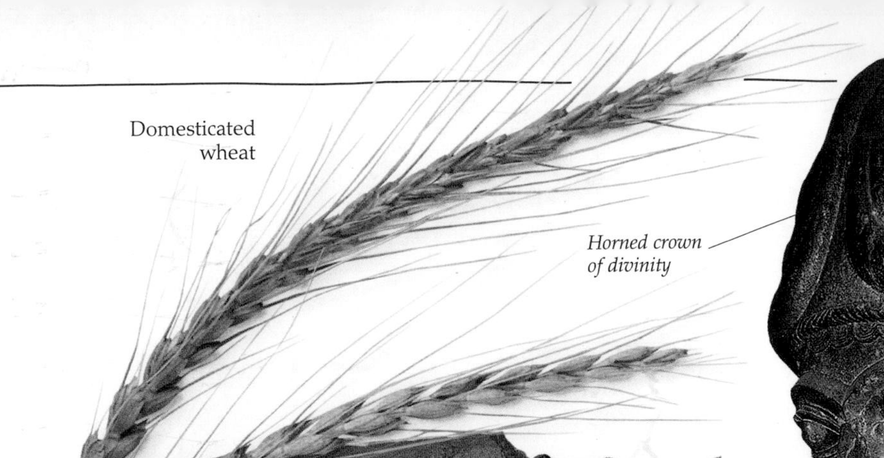

Domesticated
wheat

*Horned crown
of divinity*

ANCIENT POWER
In Mesopotamian mythology, a
lamassu was a protective spirit
with the body of winged bull
or lion and a human head. This
lamassu statue once guarded
the throne room in the palace
at Nimrud, the Assyrian
capital from 879 BCE.

Wing

THE FIRST FARMERS
These farmers gather hay in modern Iraq. In prehistoric times
an arc of fertile land (which archeologists call the Fertile
Crescent) stretched west from Mesopotamia toward the
Mediterranean coast. Inhabitants of the Fertile
Crescent grew the world's first crops and bred
the first farm animals, some time before 9500 BCE.

UNCOVERING THE PAST
This man is showing damage at Umm Al-Aqarib, an
archeological site near Umma. Tragically, the start of the
Iraq War in 2003 put a stop to
excavations and led to many
sites being looted and
damaged. The work done by
archeologists is essential for
understanding the past. They
can piece together ancient
history by studying buildings,
graves, pottery, jewelry,
statues, and ancient writings.

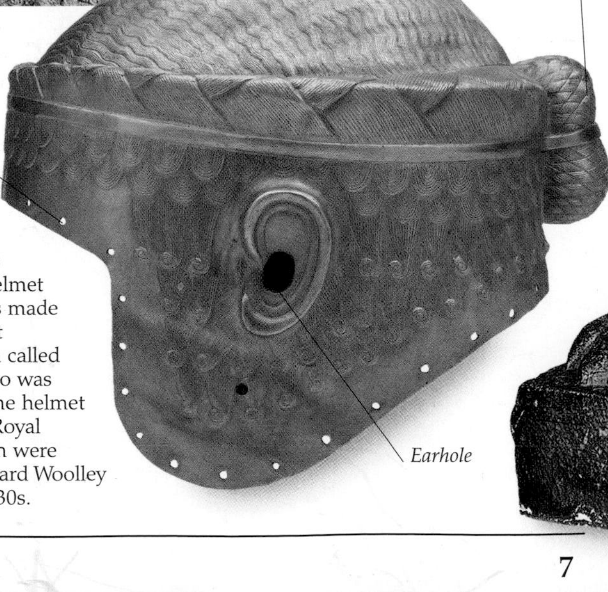

Braided bun

*Hole for attaching
the lining*

GLEAMING GOLD
This ceremonial helmet
of beaten gold was made
around 2550 BCE. It
belonged to a man called
Meskalumdug, who was
probably a king. The helmet
was found in the Royal
Tombs at Ur, which were
excavated by Leonard Woolley
in the 1920s and '30s.

Earhole

Lion's paw

Sumerian city-states

THE SMALL VILLAGES BUILT IN Mesopotamia between 7000 and 4000 BCE grew bigger. Farmers learned how to irrigate crops and grow more food. Surplus produce could be traded for items such as pottery or tools. In the southern part of the region, known as Sumer, towns and then cities developed. The cities controlled the surrounding countryside and became small states with rulers and nobles, palaces and temples. Thick, defensive walls were built around each city, for the states were often at war with each other. Leading city-states included Eridu, Uruk, Kish, Ur, Nippur, and Lagash. Soon the Sumerian way of life spread to cities as far away as Mari in the northwest and Susa in the southeast. Sumerian civilization reached its height around 2500 BCE.

RUINS AT URUK
The city-state of Uruk was occupied for about 5,000 years, reaching its peak in the third millennium BCE. In its day it was probably the biggest city in the world, with a population of about 80,000.

ANCIENT CITY-STATES
Sumer is the name given to the far south of Mesopotamia. In the third and fourth millennia BCE, the region was dominated by city-states, each built around a temple. The ancient coastline of the Gulf was farther north than today's.

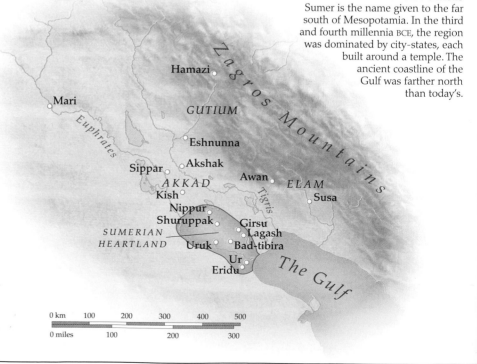

MUD BRICK
The chief building material of the Sumerians was mud brick, just as it is in modern Iraq (above). Mud is in plentiful supply and the bricks are good at keeping out the heat. Unfortunately, they crumble over time. The homes of the earliest Mesopotamians turned into dust thousands of years ago.

8

SUPPLYING THE CITY

The countryside provided food for the growing population in the cities, for the royal court, and for the priests. This scene shows oxen, sheep, goats, and donkeys being brought into Ur, probably in preparation for a banquet to celebrate a royal victory. It is one of three picture strips that decorate the "peace side" of the Standard of Ur (see page 42 for the "battle side"). Despite its name, coined by archeologist Leonard Woolley, this was probably not a standard for use in battle, but part of a musical instrument. It was made around 2500 BCE and is inlaid with lapis lazuli and shell.

THE CIVIL SERVANT

This alabaster figure from around 2400 BCE shows Ebih-Il, Superintendent of Mari. He was an important public official. The statue depicts him worshiping the goddess Ishtar and was left in her temple at Mari. Civil servants like Ebil-Il helped to introduce orderly government to the city-states of ancient Mesopotamia and, as a result, civilization could start to flourish.

A LION-HEADED EAGLE

This mythical creature is made from gold, copper, and lapis lazuli. It is marked with the name of King Mesanepada of Ur, but it was found in distant Mari. Was it a royal gift to Mari, or was it carrried off by a marauding army? Whatever its story, it is evidence of how arts, crafts, and technologies thrived in the Sumerian city-states. The Sumerians were great metalworkers, jewelers, weavers, and potters, as well as brickmakers and builders.

Lapis lazuli wing

Hands clasped in prayer

Sheep's tail

Gold base

Buckets on wheel deliver water to an aqueduct

Stone carved to look like sheepskin

PRECIOUS WATER

These medieval waterwheels in modern Syria are about a thousand years old. Waterwheels were not in use in the Middle East until about the fourth century BCE. However, throughout the history of the region, water supply and irrigation have been crucial to survival. Sumerian civilization could not have happened without the annual flooding of the great rivers and the skilled management of this precious resource.

Seat of woven reeds

Mighty rulers

The Sumerians' own name for their territory, *Ki-en-gir*, may have meant "land of the civilized lords." City-state rulers were honored with various titles, such as *en* (lord), *ensi* (governor), or *lugal* (king). The reigns of each dynasty were recorded on clay tablets known as king lists. Sumerian rulers enjoyed great power and fame and their exploits and deeds were remembered for centuries. Some rulers, such as Gilgamesh of Uruk, became legendary and their history was entangled with all kinds of myths. Sumerian kings claimed to rule by the will of the gods and therefore had to perform certain religious duties. They were also expected to be brave military commanders and builders of great cities.

Rosette with eight petals

SERVING THE GODDESS
This stone figure of Lugalkisalsi, King of Uruk and Ur in about 2350 BCE, is dedicated to the creator goddess, Nammu. The religious and political role of Sumerian kings was adopted by later Mesopotamian rulers, too.

Crescent-shaped gold earring

UR-NANSHE OF LAGASH
This stone wall carving from Girsu shows Ur-Nanshe, the first king of the powerful Lagash dynasty, in about 2480 BCE. With him are other members of the royal family. Ur-Nanshe is pictured (top left) carrying on his head a basket of clay for brickmaking. This was meant to symbolize the fact that it was he who built the city walls and temples at Lagash. He appears again (bottom right) seated on his throne. Sumerian kings lived in fine palaces, with great halls and beautiful courtyards.

Ur-Nanshe toasts the finished temple with a cup of beer

ROYAL SPLENDOR

This reconstruction shows one of the spectacular headdresses worn by Queen Puabi of Ur. The diadem is crowned by flowers, and was made from gold, lapis lazuli, and carnelian. It was worn with heavy gold earrings, dazzling collars, rich necklaces, and rings. Queen Puabi's treasures were discovered in the Royal Tombs at Ur. They show off the great wealth and prestige of the ruling families in the city-states of Sumer over 4,500 years ago.

Gold leaf shape

Bead of lapis lazuli

Eye was originally inlaid with lapis lazuli, shell, or bitumen

SYMBOL OF POWER

The limestone head of this mace is carved with lion designs and with the name of Mesilim, a king of Kish who had most of Sumer under his control around 2550 BCE. Maces were originally clublike weapons used in battle. They were so powerful that they became symbols of a king's authority and were used in public ceremonies and religious rituals.

Cuneiform inscription

Lion-headed eagle clutches captured lions in its talons

SILVER VASE

This fine silver vase was made for Entemena, son of the warrior king Enanatum. Entemena ruled the powerful city-state of Lagash from around 2455 to 2425 BCE. He built up the city walls and improved the irrigation of the fields. He also defeated the rival king of Umma in a bitter border dispute. The vase was placed in the temple of Ningirsu, who was god of farming and healing and also the patron deity of Girsu, a city within the state of Lagash. The god's symbol, the lion-headed eagle, is engraved on the side of the vase.

Copper tripod

The story of writing

EARLY PEOPLE WHO LIVED as hunters and nomads did not need written records. As the first cities arose, people began to require records of ownership, business deals, and government. The Sumerians devised the world's first script or writing system. At first they used picture symbols to represent objects such as cattle, grain, or fish. By around 3300 BCE the citizens of Uruk were using about 700 different symbols, or pictographs. These were pressed into soft clay with a stylus, leaving a wedge-shaped mark that then hardened. Over the centuries the marks developed into a script that represented sound as well as meaning. Archeologists call this cuneiform (wedge-shaped) writing. It was used by later Mesopotamian peoples, including the Akkadians, Babylonians, and Assyrians.

USEFUL TOKENS
When Mesopotamians first settled in villages and towns, they used clay tokens to record sales and receipts. The tokens were shaped as disks, triangles, cones, rectangles, and cylinders. They were kept in pouches or in clay spheres. When people pressed the tokens into the spheres, or scratched the shape of the tokens, they left marks on the spheres. These marks have been described as the very first "writing."

Bulla (archeological term for a clay sphere)

Clay token

WEDGE SHAPES
Cuneiform symbols developed because of the writing materials used. The stylus was made of a cut reed. Its tip made a wedge shape when it was pressed into clay. Combinations of wedges made different symbols. Later, cuneiform was also engraved on metal or stone.

Reed stylus

Wedge-shaped mark

Soft clay

ASSYRIAN SCRIBES
These Assyrian scribes lived in the eighth century BCE. Cuneiform-based scripts were still in use at this time across western Asia but other scripts and writing materials had also developed. One of these scribes is writing on papyrus, a kind of paper invented in Egypt and made from reeds. Later Mesopotamian scripts included the Greek and Arabic alphabets.

CYLINDER SEALS
The Mesopotamians marked their property with small cylinder seals, which were generally made of stone but sometimes of metal, wood, or ivory. The seals were usually around 1½ in (4 cm) high and engraved with designs. They could be rolled across wet clay to leave an impression. Their pictures of gods, animals, and kings reveal all kinds of details about life and beliefs in ancient Mesopotamia. Seals could also be used by traders to produce "signatures" for authorizing contracts.

Anzu the birdman being brought before Ea after stealing the Tablet of Wisdom

Impression of seal in clay

Ea, god of water and wisdom

Akkadian cylinder seal from around 2250 BCE

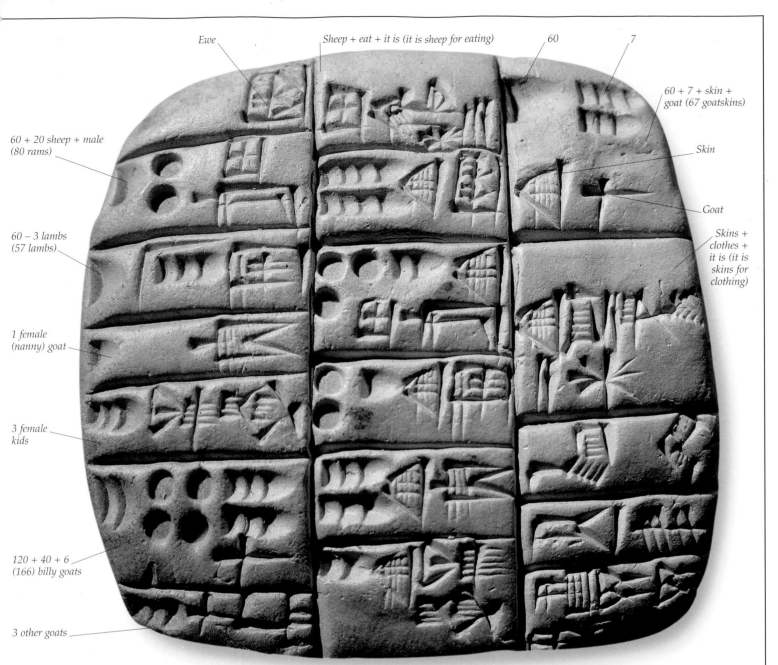

Ewe

Sheep + eat + it is (it is sheep for eating)

60

7

60 + 7 + skin + goat (67 goatskins)

60 + 20 sheep + male (80 rams)

Skin

Goat

60 − 3 lambs (57 lambs)

Skins + clothes + it is (it is skins for clothing)

1 female (nanny) goat

3 female kids

120 + 40 + 6 (166) billy goats

3 other goats

TAX RETURNS

Writing was not invented by poets, authors, or even priests, but by accountants. This clay tablet from Girsu dates from around 2350 BCE. It is written in the cuneiform script and gives details of transactions involving goats and sheep. In some cases the animals are to be sold for meat; in others, their skins are to be made into clothes. Note how numbers are totaled up from their parts (see top right). The tablet is signed by the collector of taxes. It is one of about 40,000 cuneiform tablets found in Girsu, which was once part of the kingdom of Lagash. Other tablets record distribution of barley, vegetable oil, and other commodities. The Girsu tablets offer a snapshot of ancient Mesopotamia's economy, laws, and organization.

Pictogram 3100 BCE						
Meaning	Star	Stream	Barley	Bull's head	Bowl	Head and bowl
Cuneiform sign 2400 BCE						
Cuneiform sign 700 BCE						
Meaning	God, sky	Water, seed, son	Barley	Ox	Food, bread	To eat

THE CHANGING SCRIPT

This table tells the story of writing over a period of about 2,400 years. The early picture symbols are straightforward representations of everyday objects. The cuneiform script at first imitates the pictures, but gradually becomes more and more abstract. Eventually the script is made up of symbols that can represent individual sounds as well as objects.

CRACKING THE CODE

Cuneiform script was decoded by an English soldier called Henry Rawlinson (1810–1895). He risked his life climbing a Persian rock face in order to compare inscriptions written in three ancient languages—Old Persian, Elamite, and Babylonian.

Gods and goddesses

A CRESCENT MOON
The crescent Moon was said to be the boat of the Moon god, Sin. The full Moon was his crown. The Moon god looked after the city of Ur, where he was worshiped under the name of Nanna.

THE SUMERIANS WORSHIPED MANY GODS AND GODDESSES. They believed that the stars traveling across the night sky were the cows of Sin or Nanna, the horned Moon god. Enki, the god of water and wisdom, was thought to live in an underground ocean called the Apsu. Enlil was the father of the other gods. Ninhursag, Nintu, and Nammu were all fertility goddesses, and Inanna was the goddess of love and war. Each city had its own special deity—Nippur had a great temple to Enlil, for example. The Sumerians also believed in spirits, ghosts, and demons. Later Mesopotamian peoples took up or adapted Sumerian gods, sometimes giving them new names. The Babylonians worshiped Enki as Ea, Inanna as the goddess Ishtar, and made Marduk their main god. The Assyrians were protected by Ashur and his wife Mullissu.

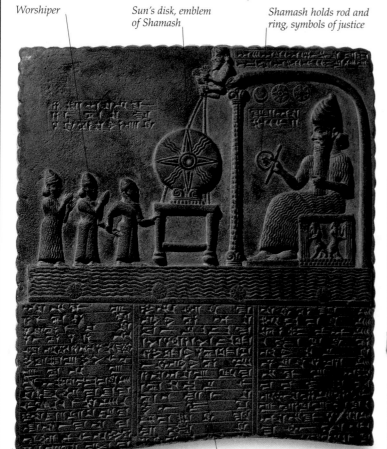

Worshiper

Sun's disk, emblem of Shamash

Shamash holds rod and ring, symbols of justice

Wavy lines depict a river or Apsu, the underground ocean

CHARIOT OF THE SUN
This tablet was excavated from Shamash's temple in Sippar. Shamash (or Utu) was the god of the Sun. He lived in the Mountain of the East. Each morning he set out in his blazing chariot and traveled across the sky to the Mountain of the West. The Sumerians believed that the Sun's rays were judgments from Shamash, coming down from the heavens to strike humankind. The god was usually shown carrying a saw, which he used to cut right from wrong.

Horned headdress, symbol of divinity

Rod and ring

QUEEN OF THE NIGHT
This clay plaque once stood in a Babylonian shrine. It is more than 3,750 years old. The figure was originally painted in red, on a black background. It probably represents Ishtar, the goddess of fertility and war. However, some experts have argued that it shows Ishtar's sister Ereshkigal, queen of the underworld, and others that it shows a female demon called Lilith.

Folded wing, symbol of the underworld

Owl, symbol of night

WATERS OF WISDOM
The Sumerians believed that the world floated on an ocean of fresh water, called Apsu. This was ruled over by Enki (later known as Ea), the god of water. In places the waters of Apsu burst through the earth to form rivers, which were the source of all wisdom. Enki therefore became the god of wisdom itself. It was Enki who warned humankind of the great flood described in Sumerian mythology and in the Bible. Enki had a special following among woodworkers, masons, and goldsmiths.

MARDUK'S DRAGON
This magnificent dragon decorated the Ishtar Gate in Babylon about 2,600 years ago. It was a symbol of the creator god Marduk. The dragon has a scaly body, a snake's head, a scorpion's tail, the feet of a lion, and the talons of a bird of prey. The dragon became associated with Marduk because the god was said to have defeated a dragonlike monster called Tiamat.

Pinecone

THE GENIE
This winged spirit or genie was one of a pair that guarded the gates of the Assyrian city of Khorsabad. The genie was believed to bless people entering the city by using a pinecone to sprinkle water from a bucket. Images of winged spirits or genies appear in many Assyrian palaces of the eighth century BCE.

Bucket of water

ETERNAL WORSHIPERS
These figures depict worshipers, who are wide-eyed with their hands clasped in prayer. The statues were made in the Sumerian city-state of Eshnunna and were left in temples. They were supposed to pray for the person who placed them there. Temples were at the center of city life and were thought to be the gods' dwelling places. Priests sacrificed animals such as rams to the gods, and tried to read the future by examining the animals' entrails.

Large eyes gaze upon statue of god

Clasped hands

City life

ONE OF THE GREATEST MOVEMENTS of people in our own times is from the countryside to the cities. This process began over 5,500 years ago in ancient Mesopotamia. People moved into the cities because these had become the center of government and trade, of religious and social life. Society was dividing into social classes. There were the rulers and priests, the administrators, the craftworkers and merchants, and the laborers. There were also large numbers of slaves, who were either prisoners of war or condemned criminals. Social divisions were reflected in the layout of the cities. At the center were temples, towering ziggurats, and luxurious royal palaces. Around these were the offices of scribes and civil servants and craft workshops. These gave way to a dense mass of housing, crisscrossed with a maze of alleys and streets. Cities were protected by massive walls with gates, and by moats. Many cities were river ports and their warehouses and wharves thronged with merchants.

BESIDE THE TIGRIS
As 19th-century archeologists discovered the remains of cities, they tried to picture how these would have looked in ancient times. This engraving shows the city of Nimrud, on the east bank of the Tigris River. The Assyrians called the city Kalhu, and it was their capital in about 880 BCE.

Decorative molding

Flat roof

Narrow window

Mud brick wall

Doorway

A MODEL HOUSE
This model house of clay is from Syria. It was made in the third millennium BCE as an offering to the gods. Ordinary Mesopotamians would have lived in houses that looked like this. Homes were rectangular, made of mud brick, and often built around a central courtyard. From the courtyard, stairs led to a flat roof, where families slept or chatted on warm summer nights. The houses were ideal for the climate—warm in winter and cool in summer. They did not need pitched roofs because there was little rainfall. The same basic house design has been in use across the Middle East for much of its history.

CITY MAP
This clay map of rivers, canals, and villages near the city of Nippur was drawn up around 1400 BCE. Cities such as Nippur depended on waterways for transportation and hygiene, and on the neighboring countryside for their food. Nippur developed from a riverside fishing village into a great Sumerian city that was occupied for thousands of years. It was dedicated to Enlil, father of the gods.

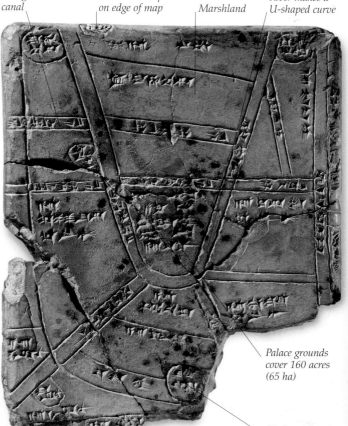

Straight canal

Marduk's temple on edge of map

Marshland

River makes a U-shaped curve

Palace grounds cover 160 acres (65 ha)

Circle represents outlying village

PALACE CARVINGS
This carving, which shows the transportation of cedar logs, is from the eighth-century-BCE palace built by the Assyrian ruler Sargon II at Khorsabad. There was a shortage of lumber in Mesopotamia, so the cedar used to build royal palaces was imported from the lands of the Phoenicians (present-day Lebanon). Logs could be towed by ships, hauled by sled, or floated down rivers.

TREES IN TOWNS
The date palm may have been cultivated in Mesopotamia as early as 6000 BCE. Dates were used as a sweetener in cooking and for making drinks. They were grown in urban plots, as they still are in modern Iraq. Figs, pomegranates, and pistachio nuts were also grown in city gardens. The water for these crops came from rivers and canals and was carried along irrigation channels. Precious water for drinking was drawn from wells or small, sunken reservoirs and stored in pottery jars.

Pomegranate

Dates

Pistachios

Full beard

Woolen tunic

CITY FASHIONS
Sumerian men wore sheepskin kilts, while the women wore long dresses and shawls made of sheepskin or wool. They wore leather shoes or sandals. Later peoples, such as these two Assyrian men from eighth-century-BCE Nineveh, wore long, woolen tunics. Both men and women wore cosmetics. Men were bearded and women wore their long hair braids.

MARKET FORCES
Copper pots go on sale in a souk or market in modern Iraq. Commerce has been the driving force of Middle Eastern cities for many thousands of years. Copper was already being traded by merchants in the ancient city-states of Sumer over 5,000 years ago.

Country life

ARCHEOLOGISTS CAN BUILD UP A VIVID PICTURE of rural life in ancient Mesopotamia by studying excavated grain and the bones of farm animals, as well as written records, pottery, and stone reliefs. Crops grown in the countryside needed to support not just the villagers but city dwellers too. Farmers had to hand over a share of their produce to government officials as taxes. Rural living was hard, particularly in the dry south, where earth dams and irrigation channels had to be maintained for watering crops. It was here that wooden plows pulled by oxen were first used, to prepare the soil for sowing. Villagers also produced cloth, baskets, and pottery. Country dwellings were made of mud brick or reeds, and each village had its own granaries and stores.

HUNTING AND FISHING
Persian fallow deer are rare today, but they were common in the time of the Sumerians, who hunted them for meat and hides. Other game included onager (a wild donkey) and gazelle, but most meat came from farm animals. The Mesopotamians also caught fish in rivers, wetlands, and along the coast.

FARM CROPS
Mesopotamian farmers grew various grain crops, which were used to make bread and beer and to provide fodder for farm animals. Vegetables included greens, peas, and beans, with onions and garlic for flavoring. Fruits that thrived in the warm climate included dates, grapes, and juicy figs. Flax, grown from about 3000 BCE, was the most important nonfood crop. It provided linseed oil and fiber for linen textiles.

Peas

Spinach

Onions

Garlic

Wild einkorn

Small seed head

Cultivated einkorn

Long, wispy husk

Cultivated emmer

GROWING GRAIN
Cereals or grain crops were first grown in the Fertile Crescent, the belt of arable (farm) land that stretched from Mesopotamia westward toward the Mediterranean. Wild grasses had small seed heads and were often difficult to thresh. By selecting only the best seeds, farmers managed to breed improved strains which offered easier harvesting, a higher yield, and better quality grain. Having reliable harvests meant that people did not have to spend all their time hunting and gathering food. It freed them up to build cities and develop the first civilizations.

Small grain

Sturdy stalk

BETTER CEREALS
Einkorn (left) and emmer (right) are two ancestors of modern wheat. The first farmers slowly improved these wild grasses through selective breeding. Emmer became the favored variety and remained the most important type of wheat for thousands of years. It is still grown in a few mountainous parts of the world. Einkorn, with its lower yields, became less popular although it, too, is still grown. Barley was another important cereal crop, which grew well in irrigated soils.

Wild emmer

Full seed head

Large grain

REED HOUSES

Large, barrel-roofed houses are still built of reeds in the wetlands of southern Iraq. The region is home to the Madan people, who may be direct descendants of the Sumerians. Their building tradition stretches back thousands of years. The *qasab* reeds grow profusely and are also used to make mats, baskets, cradles, and canoe poles. In recent years the Madan have suffered from persecution, war, and the draining of the marshes.

TENDING THE FLOCK

This small terra-cotta statue from Girsu represents a Sumerian shepherd holding a lamb. While herders in central Mesopotamia settled in villages, many in the marginal lands were seminomadic. They migrated with their flocks, taking them up into the mountains in summer and back to the valleys in winter.

Long, curved horn

Skull of a domesticated goat

COW AND CALF

This carved ivory scene of a cow suckling her calf is Syrian and dates from the ninth century BCE. Cattle were a mainstay of Mesopotamia's rural economy. They were generally kept in small herds, close to the village. They provided meat and milk, as well as hides for leather and horns for carving. Nothing was wasted, with even the dung being used as a fuel. Oxen were used for haulage and plowing the fields.

TAMING THE GOAT

Goats were first domesticated, or bred as farm animals, around 8000 BCE. Whereas wild goats had long, curved horns, the first tame ones were short-horned varieties. Goats turned out to be ideal livestock in many ways, but their ability to eat almost anything led to overgrazing. Grasses and bushes were gnawed down to the roots. Goats did better than sheep in dry, marginal lands, but those were the areas most at risk of becoming desert. Farmers raised other animals, too, including cattle, pigs, ducks, and geese.

Skull of a wild goat

Death and burial

THE EARLY PEOPLES OF MESOPOTAMIA shared similar views about the gods and about life after death. Their underworld, known as the Land of No Return, was a place of gloom and shadows. It was inhabited by the *etemmu*, winged souls of the dead whose only nourishment was dust. Much of what archeologists know about Mesopotamian burial comes from the excavation of the city of Ur in the 1920s, which revealed around 1,800 burials. Most of these were ordinary people but 16 tombs, dating from around 2600 to 2500 BCE, belonged to people of great wealth, probably royalty. They were packed with treasure.

CLAY COFFIN

Most Sumerians were buried in clay coffins like this one, or in shrouds of reed matting. Ur had a public cemetery, but people were also buried in the courtyards of family homes. The Royal Burials at Ur were in stone vaults at the bottom of deep pits. Valued possessions were placed in the graves, as offerings to the gods or for use in the afterlife.

Gold flower decorates tree

Golden beech leaf ornament

Twisted horn of lapis lazuli

Copper ear

Branch of tree or "thicket"

Tree is covered in gold leaf

TREASURES OF UR

Royal grave goods from Ur included gold and silver cups, gaming boards, and musical instruments. This elegant model goat, 18 in (46 cm) high, was made of gold, silver, shell, and deep blue lapis lazuli. It was one of a pair that Leonard Woolley named the "Rams Caught in the Thicket." They were probably part of an elaborate piece of furniture, such as a throne or offering stand.

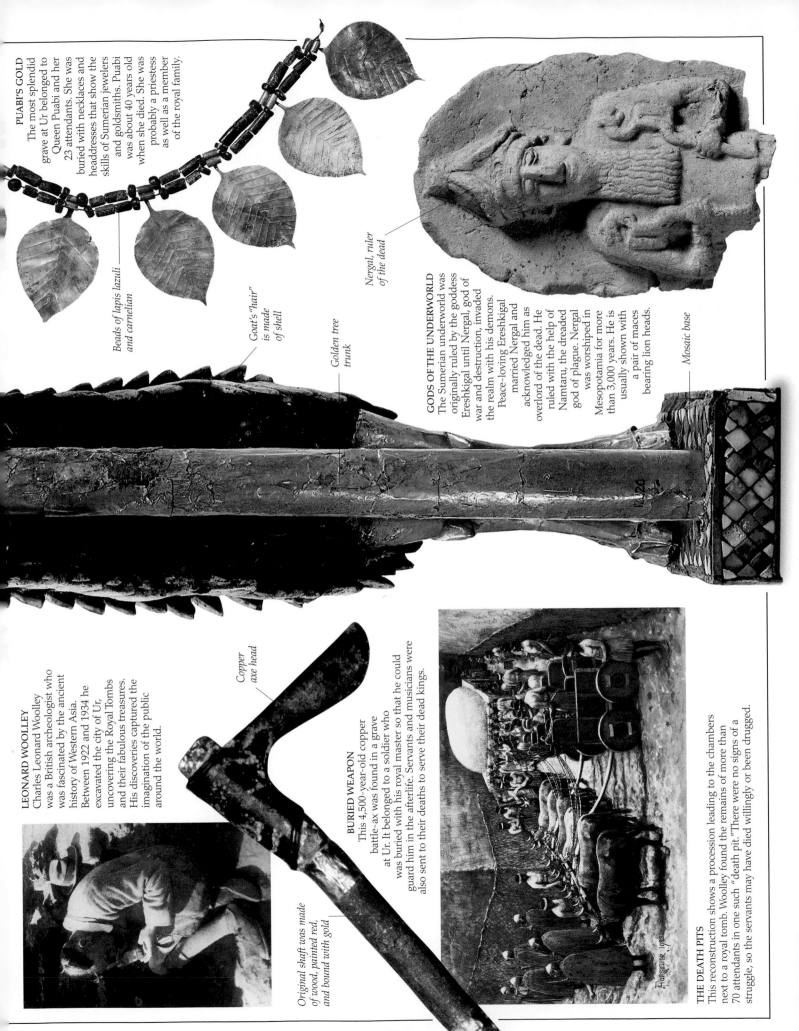

PUABI'S GOLD
The most splendid grave at Ur belonged to Queen Puabi and her 23 attendants. She was buried with necklaces and headdresses that show the skills of Sumerian jewelers and goldsmiths. Puabi was about 40 years old when she died. She was probably a priestess as well as a member of the royal family.

Beads of lapis lazuli and carnelian

Goat's "hair" is made of shell

Golden tree trunk

Nergal, ruler of the dead

GODS OF THE UNDERWORLD
The Sumerian underworld was originally ruled by the goddess Ereshkigal until Nergal, god of war and destruction, invaded the realm with his demons. Peace-loving Ereshkigal married Nergal and acknowledged him as overlord of the dead. He ruled with the help of Namtaru, the dreaded god of plague. Nergal was worshiped in Mesopotamia for more than 3,000 years. He is usually shown with a pair of maces bearing lion heads.

Mosaic base

LEONARD WOOLLEY
Charles Leonard Woolley was a British archeologist who was fascinated by the ancient history of Western Asia. Between 1922 and 1934 he excavated the city of Ur, uncovering the Royal Tombs and their fabulous treasures. His discoveries captured the imagination of the public around the world.

Copper axe head

BURIED WEAPON
This 4,500-year-old copper battle-ax was found in a grave at Ur. It belonged to a soldier who was buried with his royal master so that he could guard him in the afterlife. Servants and musicians were also sent to their deaths to serve their dead kings.

Original shaft was made of wood, painted red, and bound with gold

THE DEATH PITS
This reconstruction shows a procession leading to the chambers next to a royal tomb. Woolley found the remains of more than 70 attendants in one such "death pit." There were no signs of a struggle, so the servants may have died willingly or been drugged.

21

Akkad's rise and fall

THE LAND TO THE NORTH OF SUMER was known as Akkad. Sumer and Akkad were very similar, although the Akkadians spoke their own language. In 2334 BCE Sharrum-Kin or Sargon founded a powerful new Akkadian dynasty. Sargon was said to have been abandoned as a baby in the Euphrates River in a reed basket by his mother, a priestess. In spite of his humble beginnings, he became cupbearer to the king of Kish, seized the throne, and went on to defeat Uruk, Ur, Umma, and Lagash. Sargon's armies marched east to Elam and north to Assyria. Sargon gained control of valuable resources and trading routes and created the world's very first empire.

BULRUSH BABY
The legend of Sargon, the baby in the rush basket, crops up about 1,000 years later in the Biblical Book of Exodus. Here the baby is Moses, leader of the Hebrews.

THE FACE OF POWER
This lifelike, copper head was found at the temple of Ishtar in Nineveh. At first it was believed to represent Sargon, but because of its style of workmanship it is now thought to be his grandson, Naram-Sin, who ruled from 2254 to 2218 BCE. Naram-Sin's reign marked the height of the Akkadian Empire.

THE AKKADIAN EMPIRE
At its greatest extent, the Akkadian Empire stretched from the Gulf to the Mediterranean Sea, uniting many lands under its rule. The empire arose around 2334 BCE. It began to decline after the death of Sargon's grandson, Naram-Sin, in 2218 BCE. Uruk seized back much of Sumer, and there were attacks from Amorites and Gutians. The empire collapsed by 2160 BCE.

VICTORY TO AKKAD!

This pillar is a victory monument to Naram-Sin, who is proclaimed as king of the "four regions"—in other words, king of the whole world. The pillar was found at Susa but originally stood in the city of Sippar. It shows Naram-Sin armed with a bow and battle-ax, campaigning in mountainous country. He wears a horned headdress, which suggests that he was declared a god in his own lifetime. Later Mesopotamians blamed Naram-Sin's arrogant attitude toward the gods as the reason for Akkad's eventual decline. The king, shown twice the size of his soldiers, tramples underfoot the dying warriors of the Lullubi, a people who lived in the Zagros Mountains. In the 12th century BCE the victory pillar was carried off to Susa by Elamite invaders and damaged. It was discovered there in 1898.

Star—the pillar originally had seven—is a symbol of the gods

Naram-Sin

Akkadian standard-bearer

Defeated Lullubi

DISK OF ENHEDUANNA

In about 2300 BCE Sargon of Akkad's daughter was appointed high priestess of Nanna, the Moon god, in the city of Ur. She was given the Sumerian name Enheduanna, which means "high priestess, ornament of the heavens." Some of her writings have survived, including hymns to Inanna, goddess of love and war. Enheduanna is the first named author in history, and the first to write from a personal point of view. Later Mesopotamian princesses also served as high priestesses in Ur. Their role was to represent in person Ningal, the wife of Nanna.

Enheduanna makes an offering to the Moon god

AFTER AKKAD

This statue shows Gudea, King of Lagash, around 2100 BCE. He ruled his kingdom from Girsu, one of the Sumerian cities that grew strong again as the Akkadian Empire fell apart. After Gudea defeated the Elamites, his kingdom became prosperous from trade. Gudea was able to build 15 grand new temples. He recruited builders from far and wide, and imported cedarwood, silver, gold, and stone. The arts thrived in his reign, and many fine statues of King Gudea have survived.

Gudea seated on his throne

A NEW AGE FOR UR

This human-headed bull statue, a symbol of power and prestige, dates from the reign of Gudea. After Gudea's death the city-state of Lagash declined, and it was Ur's turn to have a great revival. During the rule of Ur-Nammu (2112–2095 BCE), the city of Ur and its ziggurat were completely rebuilt. Ur-Nammu also governed Uruk and Eridu and his influence spread far and wide.

Ziggurats and temples

A LASTING SYMBOL OF ANCIENT MESOPOTAMIA is the ziggurat, a massive terraced platform made of brick. It represented a mountain, stretching from earth to the heavens. The word *ziqquratu* is Assyrian and means "height" or "pinnacle." Ziggurats looked similar to the stepped pyramids of ancient Egypt, which were used as royal tombs, but they served a different purpose. Like the ancient pyramids of Central America, ziggurats formed part of sacred precincts, which were thought to be the earthly dwelling places of the gods. These precincts contained great temples as well as ziggurats. The ziggurats themselves had small temples or shrines on top, reached by long stairways. Temple platforms were being built at Eridu as early as 5000 BCE, but the great age of ziggurat building began in the reign of Ur-Nammu (2112–2095 BCE).

ANCIENT SITES
This crumbling tower is all that remains of Borsippa's ziggurat. Archeologists have identified 32 ziggurat sites. Some of the structures are still impressive, but many have been heavily eroded by thousands of years of wind and sand.

Arrow, symbol of Marduk

Lightning, symbol of Adad, the weather god

King Marduk-zakir-shumi

Ibni-Ishtar, a priest

TEMPLE RECORDS
This stone monument from around 850 BCE records a grant of land, houses, and temple income to a priest. Symbols of the gods serve as a reminder that they oversaw all earthly transactions. Temples, the homes of the gods, also housed important records.

ZIGGURAT DESIGN
These images of ziggurats were pressed into clay by a cylinder seal. Most ziggurats had between two and seven levels. Many were built on top of previous structures, which were considered too sacred to demolish. The monuments could be seen from a great distance across the flat landscape. On some ziggurats each story was painted a different color; others were brilliant white.

THE ZIGGURAT OF UR
Ur's ziggurat was dedicated to the Moon god, Nanna. Parts of its lower two levels have survived and been restored. The monument was raised by the great ruler Ur-Nammu and completed by his son Shulgi.

Sun-dried mud bricks were faced with fired bricks

Ceremonial stairway

Ziggurat's base was 205 ft (62.5) by 141 ft (43 m)

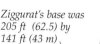

Bare head is
a sign of piety

Basket of dirt, to
make the first brick
of the temple

Offering of flowers
to the deity

TEMPLE RITUALS
A pious worshiper in a
religious procession carries a
stem of flowers in bud as an
offering to the god of the city's
ziggurat. His hand is raised,
ready to hail the god before
kneeling in reverence.

HONOR TO THE BUILDER
This small statue was placed as an offering to
the Moon god, Nanna, in the temple at Ur. It
depicts King Ur-Nammu, the ruler who built
the temple. Ur-Nammu was a pioneer of
ziggurat design and also raised ziggurats
at Eridu, Nippur, and Uruk. He was the
founder of the third dynasty at Ur and
restored the power of that city.

THE TOWER OF BABEL
The Bible tells how the descendants of Noah
quarreled when building the so-called Tower
of Babel. The tower in the tale may have been
inspired by the seven-story ziggurat at Babylon
known as the Etemenanki (meaning "the
foundation of Heaven and Earth"). This vision
of the tower dates from 1563. It was painted by
the Flemish artist Pieter Brueghel the Elder.

Ziggurat may have had three
levels, with a shrine on top

Games, music, and sports

THERE IS MORE TO CIVILIZATION than cities, government, and massive monuments. The ancient Mesopotamians were great lovers of poetry, art, and music. Public art was on a grand scale. Statues glorified rulers and famous battles. Music was played on state occasions, or in temples for the glory of the gods. However, ordinary people in towns and villages would have enjoyed informal music, dance, storytelling, sporting events, and games. The Mesopotamians liked to have a good time, and their children must have enjoyed swimming in the rivers in the heat of summer, or playing with hoops, rattles, spinning tops, jump ropes, and toy weapons.

Limestone hedgehog

HEDGEHOG CART
This model hedgehog, carved from limestone, sits on wheeled cart, 2½ in (6.5 cm) long. There was originally another animal placed behind it. The hedgehog could have been a child's toy or an offering to the gods. It dates from around 1250 BCE and was found at the Elamite city of Susa, near the temple of the city's god, Inshushinak. A lion on wheels was also discovered at Susa.

Working wheel of bituminous stone

Board made of shell, bone, lapis lazuli, limestone, and red paste

Set of seven dark counters for one player

Indent on table for score pegs

Start for first player

Six-sided die

Finish for first player

Start for second player

Finish for second player

GAMING BOARD
This glass game board is more than 3,000 years old. It came from Babylon. The Mesopotamians loved games of chance. Dice, made of bone, clay, or stone and numbered one to six, were used in many games. The world's oldest known dice were found at Tepe Gawra, near the modern city of Mosul, and date from about 2750 BCE. Gambling games were also played with disks, sticks, and knucklebones.

Shared central row

Set of seven light counters for one player

THE ROYAL GAME OF UR
This is the oldest board game in the world, and one of the most beautiful. It was found in Ur and made before 2600 BCE. The rules were similar to backgammon's. A throw of the dice decided who went first. That player put a counter on his or her start square then threw the dice to see how many squares to move. The goal was to race all seven counters along a set path around the board, then bear them off at the finish. Landing on an opponent's counter knocked it off the board so that it had to start again, but this could only happen when counters were moving along the central, shared row of squares.

SWEET MUSIC

This 4,500-year-old lyre was discovered in one of the graves in the Royal Cemetery at Ur. It had a silver shell and a wooden core, but the wood had rotted away. Archeologists were able to reconstruct it with the help of photographs taken at the site. The lyre is beautifully decorated with a bull's head and inlays of lapis lazuli and shell. No one can be sure what sort of sound the lyre produced, but cuneiform texts show that the Mesopotamians had their own musical theories about scales and tuning.

THE DRUMMERS

This fragment of a vase from the end of the third millennium BCE shows a group of Sumerian musicians with an enormous drum. Other popular instruments included kettledrums, smaller hand drums, cymbals, reed pipes, clay whistles, flutes, lutes, and harps. Musicians were taught at temple schools. Enki, god of water, was also revered as the god of music.

SPORTING CONTESTS

This terra-cotta plaque is the earliest known representation of a boxing match. It was found at Eshnunna (modern-day Tell Ashmar) and is around 4,000 years old. Wrestling was another popular sport in Mesopotamia. In the story of Gilgamesh (see page 48), the king is challenged to a wrestling match in the street by Enkidu the wild man.

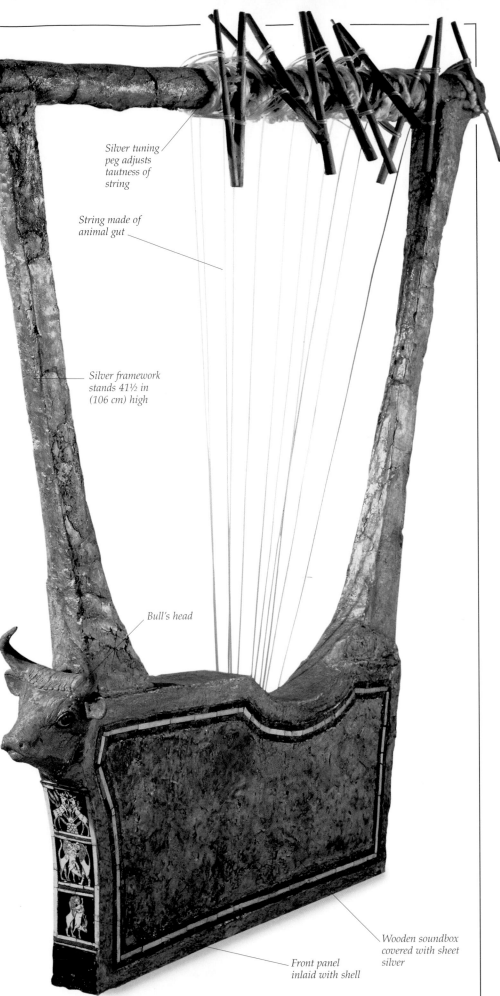

Silver tuning peg adjusts tautness of string

String made of animal gut

Silver framework stands 41½ in (106 cm) high

Bull's head

Wooden soundbox covered with sheet silver

Front panel inlaid with shell

Crafts and technology

THE MESOPOTAMIANS MASTERED many technologies and crafts at an early point in their history. They were molding clay into simple pots by the eighth millennium BCE. Some time before 3500 BCE, they invented the potter's wheel, which made pottery production far more efficient. Vessels were shaped by expert potters on the rotating wheel, then fired (baked hard) in dome-shaped kilns. The Middle East pioneered metalworking, too. Copper ore was being smelted and the molten copper poured into molds as early as the fourth millennium BCE. By 3000 BCE, metalworkers were mixing tin with the copper to produce the tough alloy called bronze. This technique was first developed in Anatolia, but soon spread to Mesopotamia with the growth in the trade in tin. Textile production was another area of technological progress. Using low, horizontal looms, women wove cloth from wool, then linen, and, from the eighth century BCE, cotton.

Delicate chain of gold links

Blue lapis lazuli from the Afghan highlands

Reddish-brown carnelian with carved ridges

GOLD, GREEN, RED, AND BLUE
This beautiful necklace, with its rich gemstones and exquisite gold work, measures (8 in) 20 cm across. It was made around 1300 BCE by skilled craftworkers in the Assyrian city of Ashur. Jewelry was worn by both men and women and indicated status and wealth. However, it was more than just a fashion item. Gems were also believed to ward off sickness and protect the wearer from evil spirits.

Pomegranate-shaped carnelian bead

Malachite may have come from Israeli mines

Stylized birds decorate the rim

THE POTTER'S ART
This beaker comes from the Elamite city of Susa and was made nearly 6,000 years ago. It is painted with bold geometric patterns. Over the centuries, potters learned to decorate pots with paint, slips (patterns made from watery clay), imprints, and engravings. Glazed finishes were perfected by about 1500 BCE. Pottery styles varied over time. When archeologists find shards of pottery, the style helps them to date the site.

Traces of decorative yellow glaze

Hand-painted geometric design

Carving originally
decorated a piece
of furniture

Hair styled in
the Egyptian
fashion

Decorative
gold setting
holds stone

DECORATIVE IVORY
This ivory carving from
Nimrud shows a woman
gazing from a window. It
is about 2,800 years old
and was the work of a
Phoenician craftworker
at the time of the Assyrian
empire. Elephant tusks were
imported from North Africa or from India.
Ivory work often included other skills such
as inlaying gemstones, gilding, or staining.

Clear quartz
or rock crystal

TEMPLE SPLENDOR
The beauty of Sumerian
temple design can be
imagined from this fine
column, which stood at
Tell Al-Ubaid, near Ur, in
about 2300 BCE. It was
one of several in front of
the temple of Ninhursag,
the goddess of childbirth.
The column was made of
a palm trunk that had
been coated in sticky
bitumen, and then faced
with a geometric mosaic.

SPINNING YARN
This modern Bedouin is spinning wool
in just the same way that Sumerian
women did more than 4,000 years
ago. In her right hand she holds a
whirling weight called a drop
spindle. The spindle's spiked
end pulls out the fibers and
twists them into thread.

Tiles made of
mother-of-pearl,
pink limestone,
and black shale

Drop spindle
is weighted so
it spins

Sheep's
wool

THE BRICKMAKERS
The Mesopotamians made bricks by putting wet mud
into rectangular, open-bottomed molds. They lifted
away the molds and left the bricks to bake and harden
in the hot sun. By about 3500 BCE brickmakers had
adopted the potter's technique of firing the clay
in kilns, and later they manufactured glazed bricks.
Fired bricks were durable and waterproof, and were
used for facing ziggurats and important buildings.
Most houses continued to be built of sun-dried brick.

Column stood
3¾ ft (115 cm) high

The rise of Babylon

BABYLON IS FIRST MENTIONED more than 4,300 years ago, as a city of the Akkadian Empire. By 1900 BCE it had been taken over by the Amurru (or Amorites), a nomadic people from the deserts to the west. They knew little of farming, let alone building, but they soon adapted to the urban way of life. Babylon became the most civilized of cities, at the hub of a growing empire. Its greatest ruler was King Hammurabi, who reigned from 1792 to 1750 BCE. At this time Babylon may have been the largest city in the world, with a population of more than 200,000. For centuries it remained a center of religion and trade. The two were closely linked, as the temples were also wealthy businesses. In 1595 BCE Babylon was attacked by Hittites, and the city later fell to Kassites and Assyrians. It did not become the capital of a great empire again until 626 BCE (see page 52).

Sun god Shamash gives the law to Hammurabi

LAWS WRITTEN IN STONE
This black pillar listed all the laws of Babylon, and the punishments for breaking them. They were displayed for all to see and carved in stone, to show that they were unchanging. The pillar stood 7½ ft (2.25 m) tall and was erected by Hammurabi around 1760 BCE. Although it is not the earliest legal code known in Mesopotamia, it is the most complete. It is one of the most important monuments to survive from the ancient world.

SOCIETY'S RULES
This clay plaque probably depicts a married couple. Marriage was one aspect of daily life that was governed by Hammurabi's laws. There were rules on dowries, violence, unfaithfulness, and divorce. Men enjoyed greater freedoms than women. Hammurabi's legal code also dealt with children, slavery, land ownership, business, taxes, professional misconduct, robbery, and murder.

Cresent moon, symbol of the Moon god, Sin

Serpent of the underworld

Eight-pointed star, symbol of the fertility goddess, Ishtar

Turtle, symbol of Ea, god of water and wisdom

Headdresses represent the great gods, Anu and Enlil

Dragon, symbol of Marduk

The dog of Gula, goddess of healing

Shrine supports the gods above

SYMBOLS OF THE GODS

This carved boulder records the granting of farmland in south Babylonia to a man called Gula-eresh. It specifies the land's area, boundaries, and value, and the names of the surveyor, the governor who granted the land, and two of his officials. Symbols of the gods protect the monument, and the text includes a curse on anyone who damages it. Public records like this were introduced by the Kassites, an eastern people who ruled Babylon from about 1415 to 1154 BCE. Like the Amorites before them, they soon adopted the old Babylonian way of life.

Solar disk, symbol of the Sun god, Shamash

Wedge shape represents Nabu, god of writing

Scorpion represents Ishara, a goddess of love

102 485

Land registration details

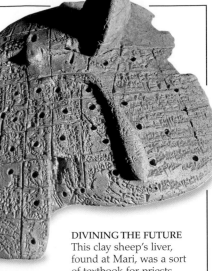

DIVINING THE FUTURE

This clay sheep's liver, found at Mari, was a sort of textbook for priests. The Babylonians believed that the gods revealed the future in the entrails of sacrificed animals. Priests checked liver omens before starting anything important, such as new construction work. The model tells how to interpret the presence of blemishes in different places on the liver.

Female goddess figure

Loop from which pendant can be hung

Mold is 93½ in (9 cm) long and 2½ in (6 cm) wide

POCKET-SIZED JEWELRY MAKER

This is half of a stone mold used for making trinkets. It comes from Sippar and dates from 1900 BCE or earlier. The jeweler poured in molten metal, probably lead, and left it to harden. Similar molds were used to produce silver and gold work.

HAMMURABI'S KINGDOM

In 1792 BCE Babylon controlled lands around the Euphrates River, including the cities of Sippar and Kish. By 1760 BCE Hammurabi had pushed the limits of his empire north to Mari and south to Ur.

Ashur
Mari
Tigris
Zagros Mountains
Euphrates
BABYLONIA
Eshnunna
Sippar
Kutha
Babylon
Kish
Nippur
Adab
Susa
Isin
Girsu
Uruk
Lagash
Larsa
Ur
The Gulf

| 0 km | 100 | 200 | 300 | 400 | 500 |
| 0 miles | 100 | 200 | 300 |

ALONG THE EUPHRATES

Babylon was built on the east bank of the Euphrates. The river was a lifeline for the city and for its first empire, providing water for people and crops. Hammurabi was a great builder of canals and waterways. Workers had to dredge the canals regularly so that they did not block up with silt from the rivers.

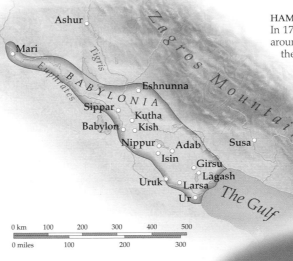

Learning and scholars

THE EARLY CIVILIZATIONS OF MESOPOTAMIA made astonishing advances in scholarship and learning—in astronomy, mathematics, medicine, geography, and architecture. In these early cities and empires we see the first glimmerings of information technology. Shelves of clay tablets packed with economic information and records were unearthed at Ebla, a city in Syria. The Ebla archive dates to around 2350 BCE and could be called the world's earliest "library." At Nineveh, in the seventh century BCE, the Assyrian ruler Ashurbanipal founded a spectacular library that contained a wide range of literary, religious, scholarly, and medical texts from all over Mesopotamia.

This square contains eight triangles

LEARNING TO WRITE
This is a school exercise book in the form of a clay tablet, written by a trainee scribe nearly 4,000 years ago. The scribe copied the writing from an example by a teacher or older pupil. The name for a school was *edubba* ("tablet house"). Pupils also learned to trim their reed stylus and make clay tablets.

𒁹	1	𒀹	2	𒁹𒁹𒁹	3	𒃻	4
𒐊	5	𒐋	6	𒐌	7	𒐍	8
𒐎	9	𒌋	10	𒌋𒁹	11	𒌋𒀹	12
𒌋𒁹𒁹𒁹	13	𒌋𒃻	14	𒌋𒐊	15	𒌋𒐋	16
𒌋𒐌	17	𒌋𒐍	18	𒌋𒐎	19	𒌋𒌋	20
𒌍	30	𒐏	40	𒐐	50	𒁹	60

NUMBER CRUNCHING
The Mesopotamians were writing down numbers over 5,000 years ago. Like their "letters," the numerals were wedge-shaped symbols. The same symbol was used for "1" and "60," because the main counting system had 60 as its base. It was used alongside a decimal system, based on the number 10. There was no sign for zero.

Cuneiform text identifies shapes above (four triangles and a square) and asks for their areas

PROBLEMS TO SOLVE

This 3,800-year-old clay tablet is a school textbook of geometry problems. The writing underneath each picture describes the shapes inside the square and asks the reader to find their areas. In each example the square's sides are 60 rods long—the equivalent of 1,180 ft (360 m). During the first Babylonian empire, students were using multiplication tables and calculating squares, square roots, cubes, and cube roots. Today's mathematicians still use the Old Babylonian counting system, based on multiples of 60, when they divide the circle into 360 (6 x 60) degrees.

Mechanical hand moves 6 degrees to mark each minute

SIXTY MINUTES...

The Babylonian way of counting based on the unit of 60 is known as the sexagesimal system. It survives in the 60-minute hour and 60-second minute, as well as in modern geometry.

Official weighing tribute

Balance scale

Gift of treasure for King Ashurnasirpal II

WEIGHTS AND MEASURES

This stone relief from Nimrud shows scales being used for weighing. It dates from the ninth century BCE. Weights were based on a unit called the *mina*, which was about 18 oz (500 g). The Mesopotamians had other units of measurement for volume, area, and length, which were standardized from around 2100 BCE.

MASTER BUILDERS

This brickwork at Choga Zanbil (the Elamite city of Dur Untash, now in Iran) dates from around 1250 BCE. The Mesopotamians were the first to use the arch and the column. These structures gave architects the freedom to simultaneously span space and support weight. The great ziggurats are also evidence of how the Mesopotamians used math to make progess in architecture.

Potash, a purgative to get rid of toxins through vomiting

MESOPOTAMIAN MEDICINE

Illness was believed to be a punishment from the gods. It could be diagnosed by an *ashipu*, an expert in magic and divinity, or by an *asu* or physician, who learned the effectiveness of certain herbs and remedies. While some of these could only have had an imagined effect, others are still valued today for their medicinal properties.

Thyme, an antiseptic

Pine nuts for ulcers

Saffron for depression

Juniper, an antiseptic and purgative

UNLUCKY ECLIPSE

Priests observed the movements of the Sun, Moon, planets, and stars in order to predict the future. Eclipses of the Sun were a sign of ill omen. By about 500 BCE these astrologers could accurately predict when eclipses would occur.

Sunflower seeds for coughs

Wider horizons

BEYOND THE LAND OF THE TWO RIVERS, there had always been contact with other peoples, through warfare, migration, and trade. During the second millennium BCE these peoples played an important part in Mesopotamian history. The Hittites were a warlike people from Anatolia who established a kingdom called Hatti and attacked Babylon in 1595 BCE. The Hurrians, who settled in northern Mesopotamia, founded a powerful kingdom called Mittani, which conquered many lands around 1480 BCE. The armies of Egypt also marched into Asia in the 1400s BCE. Discoveries at Tell al-Amarna have revealed close relations between ancient Egypt and Mesopotamia.

Obelisk has ziggurat-like, stepped top

Cuneiform script

THE AMARNA LETTERS
In 1887, archeologists discovered 382 clay tablets at Tell al-Amarna in Egypt. Written in the Akkadian language, they date to just before 1350 BCE. They include diplomatic letters of friendship, like this one from King Tushratta of Mittani to Amenhotep III of Egypt. Alliances were sealed with royal marriages and gifts of ships, oils, and lumber.

Inked footnote added in Egyptian hieratic script

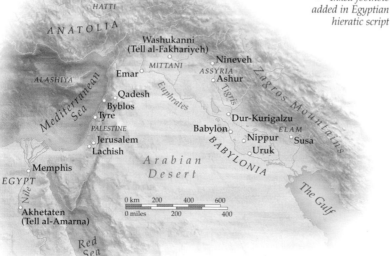

Map labels: Hattusas, HATTI, ANATOLIA, Washukanni (Tell al-Fakhariyeh), MITTANI, Nineveh, ALASHIYA, Emar, ASSYRIA, Ashur, Zagros Mountains, Qadesh, Euphrates, Tigris, Byblos, Tyre, PALESTINE, Dur-Kurigalzu, Jerusalem, Babylon, ELAM, Lachish, Nippur, Susa, Memphis, Arabian Desert, BABYLONIA, EGYPT, Nile, Uruk, The Gulf, Akhetaten (Tell al-Amarna), Red Sea, Mediterranean Sea

0 km 200 400 600
0 miles 200 400

Silver, gold, tin, bronze, ivory, and ebony from northwest Syria

Hittite tribute of silver, gold, lead, copper, ivory, and cypress wood

THE BIG PICTURE
The second millennium BCE saw dramatic changes across Western Asia. Egypt extended its territory north into Palestine, and its armies even reached the Euphrates. At the same time, the Hittites moved south. They clashed with the Hurrian kingdom of Mittani around 1480 BCE, and fought the Egyptians at the indecisive Battle of Qadesh in 1274 BCE.

34

THE BLACK OBELISK

This column or obelisk was made for the Assyrian king Shalmaneser III, who reigned from 858 to 824 BCE. It stands 6½ ft (2 m) high and shows tributes of wild animals being brought from across his empire. The king in the second row down is Jehu, who ruled Israel from 842 to 815 BCE, and who is mentioned in the Bible. From the earliest times Mesopotamia had strong links with the peoples whose story is told in Jewish, Christian, and Muslim scriptures. The patriarch Abraham may have been born in Ur in about 2000 BCE.

HITTITE WARRIOR

Fierce warriors, the Hittites were famous for their use of wheeled war chariots. They were also skilled metalworkers, and the first people to use iron weapons. Their attack on Babylon in 1595 BCE led to the fall of the first Babylonian Empire. After 1200 BCE Hittite power in the region began to decline.

Tribute from northwest Iran includes a Bactrian camel

Egyptian-style kohl-rimmed eye

Ivory originally stained with dyes

ELAMITES AND KASSITES

This relief shows an Elamite woman spinning yarn. During the second millenium BCE the Elamites became powerful to the east of Mesopotamia around Susa (now in Iran). Another eastern people, the Kassites, moved into southern Mesopotamia. By 1450 BCE the Kassites had gained control over most of the old Sumerian cities.

THE FIGHTING PHARAOH

This colossal statue at Abu Simbel in southern Egypt is 65½ ft (20 M) high. It commemorates the pharaoh Ramses II, who ruled from 1279 to 1213 BCE. Ramses II fought the Hittites at Qadesh but had to make a treaty with them in 1259 BCE. He needed allies in the face of the growing power of the Assyrians.

BEAUTY IN IVORY

This smiling face, known as the Mona Lisa of Nimrud, is one of thousands of ivory carvings discovered at the Assyrian capital. The pieces, probably tributes paid to Assyrian kings, date from 800 to 700 BCE and show how cultural influences came from far and wide. Although some of the styling looks Egyptian, the ivories were made by Phoenicians and Syrians. Many pieces were gilded or inlaid with gems.

Trade and commerce

MESOPOTAMIA WAS A CENTER OF TRADE from the time of its earliest settlement. The region had few resources of its own, but it was a crossroads for vital trading links between Central Asia, Afghanistan, Persia, Arabia, Egypt, the eastern Mediterranean, and Anatolia. More than 10,000 clay tablets have been found at Kanesh in Turkey, recording trade between Anatolia and northern Mesopotamia. Goods were carried between each trading post or *karum* by donkey or riverboat. Profits came not only from the goods themselves but from the taxes levied along the way. Cities such as Mari grew wealthy from this revenue.

DOING A DEAL
Two Syrian merchants agree on price and delivery of goods. Contracts were recorded on clay tablets and authenticated by the cylinder seals of the two parties. Payment was made in silver, in units called shekels. A shekel weighed around ¼ oz (8 g).

LION WEIGHTS
This bronze lion was a weight used by Assyrians in 700 BCE. It weighed 15 *minas*, the equivalent of 16 lb (7.5 kg), and was part of a set ranging from 2 oz (50 g) to 45 lbs (20 kg). Weights measured not only goods, but also the silver used as money.

GOODS FOR A KING
This bronze band is from the Balawat Gates (see page 50). The top half shows Phoenician merchants shipping goods as tribute to Shalmaneser III, who ruled Assyria from 858 to 824 BCE. The merchants give these goods in return for the right to remain free. The bottom part of the band shows what happened to people who did not pay their dues. The Assyrians are attacking the town of Hazazu, in Syria, and have captured and enslaved its inhabitants.

Phoenician cargo ships leaving the port of Tyre, in Lebanon

EXPORTS AND IMPORTS
Materials that were exported from the lands of Mesopotamia included silver, barley and wheat, oils, wool, and textiles. Imports included tin, copper, gold, black diorite, blue lapis lazuli from what is now Afghanistan, gleaming white pearls from the Gulf coast, red carnelian, ivory, and pottery from as far away as the Indus valley. Copper came from Magan, on the tip of the Arabian peninsula. This became a key staging post for trade with India, as did Dilmun (modern Bahrain).

Lapis lazuli

Silver

Pearls

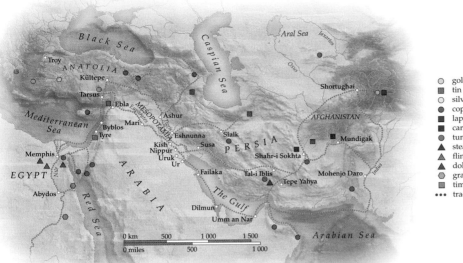

THE TRADING NETWORK
Some of the raw materials used in Mesopotamia had traveled from mines that were more than 600 miles away. No merchant operated across the whole region. Goods changed hands at various trading posts along the way.

gold
tin
silver
copper
lapis lazuli
carnelian
turquoise
steatite
flint
dolerite
granite
timber
••• trade route

CEDAR OF LEBANON
Lumber was scarce in both Mesopotamia and Egypt, so it became a precious commodity. Lebanese cedar was the most valued wood of all, used to build ships, palaces, and temples. It still grows in Lebanon today, although it has become very rare. It is also found in southern Turkey and western Syria.

*Assyrian king,
Shalmaneser III*

*Tribute bearers carry bales
of cloth, upturned cauldrons,
and trays of jewelry*

*Enslaved inhabitants of
Hazazu are escorted away,
perhaps to be sold*

TRADE AND CRAFTS
This beautiful necklace of carnelian and lapis lazuli comes from the city-state of Kish and was made in about 2500 BCE. The raw materials may have been imported from distant lands, but the craftwork is distinctly Mesopotamian.

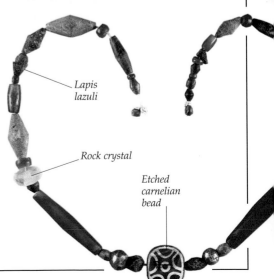

*Lapis
lazuli*

Rock crystal

*Etched
carnelian
bead*

Gold

Carnelian

Transportation and travel

THE FIRST ANIMALS TO BE USED FOR TRANSPORTION and haulage in Mesopotamia were oxen, onagers (a type of wild pony), and donkeys. Horses were not introduced until around 2000 BCE, and camels not until 1500 BCE. The first vehicles were simple wooden sleds, dragged along the ground. At some point between 3500 and 3200 BCE there was a momentous technological breakthrough—the invention of the wheel. Wheeled vehicles appeared around the same time as the potter's wheel, the spinning horizontal board used for shaping clay, but it seems that the two inventions arose independently. The invention of wheeled vehicles made it easier to move bulky or heavy objects and also people. As wheel designs improved, faster, lighter vehicles such as war chariots appeared. Roads were built from the 2000s BCE. King Shulgi of Ur, who reigned from 2094 to 2047 BCE, was said to have celebrated the new road from Ur to Nippur by running there and back in a day, with a stop for a banquet halfway! Assyrian roads, built around 800 BCE for royal messengers, had relay posts every 20 miles (30 km) or so.

COVERED TRANSPORTATION
The first vehicles were really just sleds to which wheels had been attached. This clay model goes a stage further. It represents a covered wagon, and was made in Syria more than 4,000 years ago. Early wagons traveled no faster than walking pace, but at least they took the strain out of transporting heavy goods.

Planked wheel

Cross-piece fastens planks

Axle allows wheel to turn

WAGON WHEELS
Wood for making wheels was a luxury in Mesopotamia. The shortage of large tree trunks for making solid wheels led to an alternative design. Two or three narrow plank sections were joined together to make up a wheel. The trouble was that these were very heavy, so from about 2000 BCE wheels were made with sections removed. This meant that the rim had to be strengthened with bars or spokes.

Spoke strengthens the wheel

Cross-bar

Axle

Hollow area inside rim makes wheel lighter and faster

Cross-bar wheel with spokes

HIGH-SPEED CHARIOTS
The first chariots, used for warfare or hunting, had wooden wheels and were heavy, slow, and difficult to maneuver. Fast, light, spoke-wheeled chariots were developed from about 2000 BCE. Great masters of charioteering skills included the Hittites and the Assyrians.

Assyrian hunting chariot

DECORATIVE HARNESS

This Sumerian rein ring is part of a harness found among the Royal Tombs at Ur. About 4,500 years old, it is made of gold and silver and is decorated with the figure of an onager. However, the reins were used to control oxen, not onagers. The ring was found among the bones of two oxen in front of a sled. Sleds were used for ceremonies for some time after the invention of the wheel.

Onager made of electrum (gold and silver alloy)

Reins for the ox were threaded through each ring

Fixture for wooden pole attached to the sled

Frame of woven reeds, coated with tar

RIVERBOATS

The *quffa* is a small round boat of wickerwork and reeds that is still used on the Tigris and Euphrates. The basic design has not changed in thousands of years. Waterways were important for transportion. The simplest boats were rafts on inflated goatskins. Boats with sails appeared as early as 4000 BCE. Bitumen, a tar that occurred naturally along the Euphrates, was used for waterproofing.

Phoenician shield

THE SEAFARERS

This Assyrian stone relief from the ninth century BCE shows a Phoenician war galley. Armed warriors man the upper deck, their shields ranged along the side of the ship. Two banks of oars power the vessel forward to the attack. A ship like this would have been about 100 ft (30 m) long. The Phoenicians were the great seafarers of the ancient world and may even have been the first to sail all the way around Africa.

Oar from lower bank

Oar from upper bank

DESERT CARAVAN

Camels became a common sight in Mesopotamia from the first millennium BCE. They were used as transportation in warfare as well as for carrying traded goods. Camels could also supply skin for leather, hair for textiles, meat, milk, and dung for fuel. The single-humped camel or dromedary came originally from Arabia. The two-humped or Bactrian camel came from central Asia. Camels are ideal for desert travel. Their bodies are adapted to cope with walking over sand dunes or being blasted by dust storms. Above all, they can travel for long periods without water.

The Assyrian Empire

TIGLATH-PILESER III
During his reign (745–727 BCE), Tiglath-pileser III made Assyria powerful once again through a series of remarkable conquests. His armies stormed across northern lands and down the Mediterranean coast, adding new territories to the Assyrian Empire. Tiglath-pileser III built a fine palace at the provincial city of Kalhu, the site later known as Nimrud.

THE HOMELAND OF THE ASSYRIAN PEOPLE was around the Tigris River, a long way north of Babylon. Their city of Ashur began to grow wealthy from trading with Anatolia as early as 2000 BCE. The Assyrians had few resources and little fertile land of their own, so they set out to conquer other lands. In 1120 BCE their ruler, Tiglath-pileser I, founded an empire that reached to the eastern Mediterranean. The area under Assyrian control expanded again under Sargon II, who seized power in 721 BCE. The mighty empire was finally brought down in 612 BCE, when the Babylonians destroyed its capital, Nineveh, and other major cities including Nimrud. The Assyrians are remembered in history as cruel and ruthless warriors, but they were also scholars, lovers of art, builders of magnificent cities, and loyal worshipers of their chief god, Ashur.

APES AND IVORY
Assyrian armies brought back plunder and treasure from all over the empire. Conquered rulers paid tribute in the form of valuables such as ivory, gold, lumber, camels, or horses. Exotic animals including apes, monkeys, rhinoceroses, and elephants were also sent to the Assyrian king as symbols of foreign lands under his rule.

Winged disc contains image of the supreme god, Ashur

Ashurnasirpal II carries a mace, a symbol of kingship

The Sacred Tree

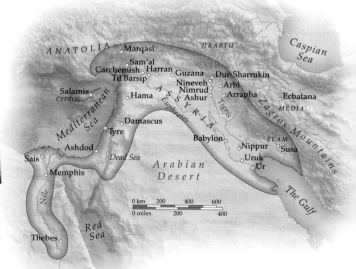

ASHURNASIRPAL II
Both figures on this alabaster wall carving represent Ashurnasirpal II, king of Assyria from 883 to 859 BCE. He was a powerful warrior who made his capital at Nimrud, known then as Kalhu. This carving decorates the Northwest Palace and shows the king in his role as high priest. He stands on each side of the Sacred Tree, a stylized palm that represents fertility and appears in many carvings at Nimrud. The Assyrians' supreme deity, the sky god Ashur, presides over the king inside a winged disk. Wall reliefs such as these would originally have been painted in bright colors.

ASSYRIAN CONQUESTS
At its height the Assyrian Empire included all of Mesopotamia, as well as parts of Anatolia, Syria, Lebanon, Cyprus, Palestine, and even Egypt, which was conquered in 671 BCE. In order to control this vast territory, Tiglath-pileser III built a system of roads, for use only by armies and royal messengers. He grasped how important roads were for maintaining military power, an idea that was later adopted by the Persians and, above all, the Romans.

WALLS OF NINEVEH

Sennacherib, who was Assyrian king from 704 to 681 BCE, made Nineveh his capital. This ancient city on the east bank of the Tigris River had 15 great gates. It was surrounded by a moat and a long, stone-built outer wall, with castlelike battlements (shown here, restored). Inside that was a very high wall of mud brick. The Assyrians knew all about city walls because they were masters of siege warfare and great builders of battering rams and assault towers.

AN ASSYRIAN SPHINX

This gilded ivory carving, found at Nimrud, dates from the late eighth century BCE. It represents a sphinx, a mythical beast with a lion's body and a human head. It wears an Egyptian headdress, but it was probably made by a Phoenician from the Mediterranean coast. The sphinx originated in Egyptian mythology, but from about 1500 BCE it also appears in Mesopotamian images.

Sphinx has head of an Egyptian pharaoh, with royal crown, headdress, and collar

Egyptian lotus or water lily

Feathered wing

Sphinx has a lion's body and tail

Lion's paw

Ancient warfare

City walls were fortified with towers and battlements

MESOPOTAMIA WAS AT WAR for most of its history. Each Sumerian city-state was constantly trying to defeat the others, as when Lagash engaged in a brutal war with neighboring Umma in 2440 BCE. Early images of battle show dense ranks of copper-helmeted Sumerian warriors carrying spears and leather shields. Warfare was not just the work of power-crazed kings, eager for glory. It resulted from growing populations desperate to control scarce resources such as water, minerals, or lumber. That need drove the creation of ever-larger empires, which had to be governed with the support of a powerful, ruthless army. In 1120 BCE, the Assyrian king Tiglath-pileser I advanced as far as the Mediterranean. The Assyrians were masters of warfare. Their tactics depended on besieging and assaulting the most important cities in enemy territory. They diverted rivers to cut off water supplies. They breached walls with huge battering rams and built high wooden towers as platforms for archers. They also slaughtered all who resisted, as an example to other cities.

WEAPONS OF WAR
This copper dagger dates from around 2500 BCE. Before this time, the Mesopotamians fought with heavy maces, slingshots, arrows, and spears. Copper weapons were later replaced with stronger ones of bronze and, later still, of iron.

CHANGING CHARIOTS
This model chariot was made in Syria. Marks on its wheels may represent spokes. After about 2000 BCE the Sumerians' trundling war wagons, hauled by onagers or asses, were replaced by lightweight chariots pulled by powerful horses. Horses were introduced into Mesopotamia by northern tribes.

Sumerian king holds spear

Prisoners paraded naked before the king

War chariot pulled by four onagers

UR ON THE MARCH
The so-called Standard of Ur (see page 9) dates from about 2500 BCE. The "battle side" is one of the earliest depictions of an army. It shows the soldiers of Ur on the march. We see the soldiers' helmets and cloaks, and their axes and spears. Each war wagon is pulled by a team of onagers. The enemy is trampled underfoot or taken captive.

Soldier is protected by body armor, a shield, helmet of iron or bronze, and leather boots

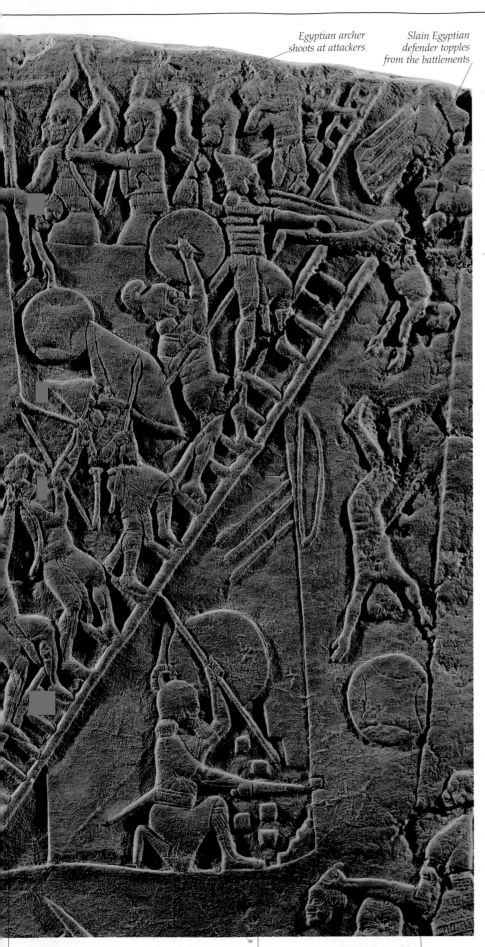

Egyptian archer shoots at attackers

Slain Egyptian defender topples from the battlements

Scaling ladder allows the Assyrians to reach the battlements

Infantryman is undermining the city walls

Shield dropped by falling Egyptian defender

ASSYRIAN ASSAULT

Troops storm a city during Ashurbanipal's campaign in Egypt in 645 BCE. This was the great age of siege warfare and the Assyrians are meeting fierce resistance as they use ladders to scale the city walls. Armies were already using iron weapons, which were extremely strong and sharp. Stone carvings at Assyrian palaces showed many brutal scenes of warfare, such as captives being impaled on stakes and defeated kings being beheaded. The Assyrians had discovered some of the most effective weapons of war and government—state terror and propaganda.

WALLS IN BABYLON

These are Babylonian ruins from the reign of King Nebuchadnezzar II (604–562 BCE). The tops of the walls, or battlements, were crenellated. The upright sections provided cover for defending archers, while the gaps in between allowed them to shoot arrows or drop stones on the attacking troops.

THE CAVALRY

This is a mounted soldier from the 10th century BCE. The future of warfare lay with horsemen who were mobile and heavily armed. Assyrian mounted archers rode in pairs. One held both sets of reins, leaving the other free to release a hail of arrows. Arrows had shafts of reeds and heads of flint, bone, or metal.

The art of hunting

MESOPOTAMIAN CIVILIZATION AROSE at the time when farming replaced hunting as the chief source of food. As the centuries passed, hunting for food still continued in wetlands, forests, and mountains. However, to the rulers in their walled cities on the plains, hunting became more of a ritual, designed to show off the king's bravery, superiority, and the favor he found with the gods. This practice continued down the ages, from the Sumerians to the chariot-riding Assyrians. The animals used in these ritual hunts had to be worthy opponents. Wild bulls or lions were often used, because they were associated with the legends of Gilgamesh (see page 48). In reality, a king needed little skill at tracking down wild animals or battling with them—the royal hunts were stage-managed affairs and the king's life was never put at risk.

THE HUNTER
A successful hunter emerges from the forest. This eighth-century-BCE Assyrian carving comes from the palace of Sargon II. The link between royalty and hunting probably goes back to the days before farming, when a tribal chief had to be a skilled hunter.

THE ROYAL LION HUNT
This stone panel comes from the palace of Ashurnasirpal II at Nimrud and shows a lion leaping at the king's chariot. Ashurnasirpal II, who reigned from 883 to 859 BCE, was an avid hunter who claimed to have killed 450 lions. On the day of the hunt, the king would leave the city and ride out to an enclosed hunting park. There, lions were released from cages and the hunt began, generally from a chariot, but sometimes on foot. The animals were killed with arrows and then offered up to the gods. The royal lion hunt remained an important occasion for Mesopotamian kings over several thousand years.

HUNTING DOGS
Mastiffs are large, powerful, and fierce breeds of dog. The ancient Mesopotamians bred them for hunting. During the royal lion hunt, mastiffs guarded the edge of the arena. Mastiffs were also used to bring down onagers or wild asses.

Two guards herd the lion toward the royal chariot but also ensure the king is never in danger

Lion has already been struck by four of the king's arrows

Hunting chariot has a lightweight, spoked wheel

LIONS AND KINGS
This ivory carving from Nimrud shows a lion attacking a Nubian boy. Lions were symbolic animals. This one may represent the brave Assyrian king conquering his enemies. In the royal hunt, the lion represented savagery, while the king represented order and protectiveness.

Teal

Mallard

Francolin

FOOD FOR THE POT
For ordinary people, hunting was not an elaborate ritual, but a way of filling the cooking pot. Archeologists often find the bones of animals that were hunted and butchered. Rabbits, deer, antelope, game birds, and waterfowl were all caught for food.

CASTING THE NET
A fisherman casts his net at Kerbala in modern Iraq. In ancient times, nets were used for snaring small game animals and birds as well as for fishing. The Sumerian word for hunting used the symbol of a net. Fishermen also used harpoons, lines, and traps. Fish from rivers and coasts were always an important source of food. They could be preserved by drying in the sun, by salting down, or by pickling.

King is armed with a bow and arrow and a sword

Charioteer whips the horses to make them gallop

Horses were introduced to pull chariots in around 2000 BCE

Slain lion is trampled underfoot by the horses

Assyrian palaces

THE ASSYRIANS BUILT AWE-INSPIRING cities. Between the ninth and seventh centuries BCE, Kalhu (now known as Nimrud), Nineveh, and Dur-Sharrukin (modern-day Khorsabad) all served as capitals of the Assyrian Empire. A series of rulers built luxurious palaces within their walls. These were magnificent buildings. Their massive gates were bound in bronze, their walls were of glazed bricks, their beams of cedar, and their roofs of other precious woods. A great courtyard would lead to a long throne room, which was guarded by colossal statues of mythical beasts. Its walls were alive with carvings of battle and hunting scenes, or with images of defeated peoples paying tribute to the great king. All were painted in brilliant colors, and designed to impress foreign rulers or ambassadors who came to pay homage. An inner courtyard would lead to the private apartments of the royal family, to the servants' quarters, and to the kitchens.

Harpist   *Severed head of the Elamite king*

Wings symbolize protective powers

Human head with divine headdress and elaborate beard

Body of a bull to symbolize strength

GUARDIAN OF THE PALACE
Lamassu statues were human-headed winged bulls or lions. These mythological creatures guarded the doors of Assyrian royal palaces. This example is from the eighth-century-BCE palace of Sargon II at Dur-Sharrukin. *Lamassu* statues were later adopted by Persian kings and appear in such palaces as Persepolis. They were believed to ward off evil spirits and were supposed to embody the various qualities of the creatures they represented, such as strength, intelligence, and courage.

Lamassu *stands more than 13 ft (4 m) tall*

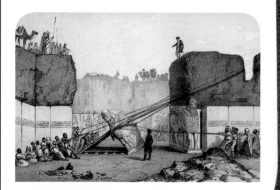

TO FOREIGN LANDS
The archeologist Austen Henry Layard explored the site of Nimrud between 1845 and 1851. Here he supervises the removal of a colossal stone statue—a winged guardian. Layard shipped the monuments he had discovered at Nimrud to the British Museum in London. The journey was perilous but successful. The rest of the world became fascinated by the treasures of ancient Mesopotamia.

Fifth leg was added to make the creature look like it was in motion

Fly swatter is used to bat flies off the food

Attendant holds date-palm fan

Queen Ashursharrat holds a cup of wine

King Ashurbanipal reclines on a couch

A VICTORY BANQUET

A carving from the North Palace at Nineveh shows King Ashurbanipal and Queen Ashursharrat feasting after the Battle of Til-Tuba in 653 BCE. Birds fly among the palms and vines. Servants fan the king and queen and cater for their every need. There is sweet music, fine food, and wine to drink—but hanging from the tree on the left is the severed head of Teumman, the defeated Elamite king. The rotting head is a grim reminder of the recent battle and a lesson to all who would challenge Assyrian supremacy.

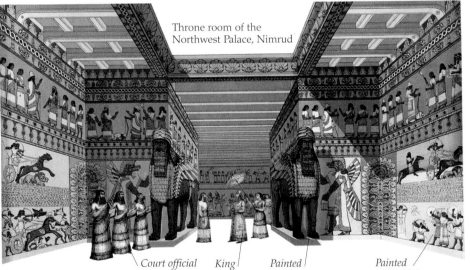

Throne room of the Northwest Palace, Nimrud

Court official *King* *Painted stone lamassu* *Painted wall relief*

ON THE MENU

The Assyrians dined on all kinds of meat, fish, and fowl, and on cheese, fruit, and bread. Foods were sweetened with honey or date syrup. Crunchy desert locusts were a delicacy. King Ashurnasirpal II once hosted a 10-day banquet that catered for 47,074 guests.

Sweet black grapes

THE ROYAL COURT

This is how the archeologist Austen Henry Layard pictured the throne room of King Ashurnasirpal II, who ruled from 883 to 859 BCE. Layard may not have been correct in every detail, but he does give some idea of the grandeur of this glittering court. The king stands at the center, flanked by his royal officials. A ceremonial parasol is held above his head.

DUR-SHARRUKIN

This engraving of 1867 shows one of the imposing towered gates into Dur-Sharrukin, as imagined by Felix Thomas, a member of the team that excavated Sargon II's palace there. Sargon II, who seized power in 722 BCE, was an Assyrian, but he named himself after the first Sargon, ruler of Akkad. He made his capital at Dur-Sharrukin, which means "the fortress of Sargon."

Gilgamesh's beauty came from the Sun god, Shamash

Hero grips vanquished lion

The epic of Gilgamesh

AN EPIC IS A GRAND TALE OF GODS AND HEROES, love and friendship, and adventures and tragedy. The epic of Gilgamesh is the world's earliest surviving work of literature. It was first written down around 2000 BCE, but the story itself is older. The hero is Gilgamesh, a superhuman king whose real-life counterpart may have reigned in the Sumerian city of Uruk around 2700 BCE. The epic tells of the king's adventures with the wild man Enkidu, sent by the gods to tame him. A wrestling match between Enkidu and Gilgamesh ended in a draw and the two became fast friends. The epic also tells how the goddess Ishtar fell in love with Gilgamesh and how, with Enkidu's help, he killed the monster Humbaba and the Bull of Heaven. After Enkidu's death, Gilgamesh set out on a quest for the secret of eternal life. He met Utnapishtim, the man who saved the world in the great flood. By the end of the epic, Gilgamesh has learned that all humans are mortal, even mighty kings.

THE WRITTEN WORD
The most complete version of the epic to survive was written on clay tablets that were found in the city of Nineveh. The tablets date from the seventh century BCE and were part of the library of King Ashurbanipal. The epic remained popular over many centuries among all the peoples of Mesopotamia, as well as with invaders such as the Hurrians and the Hittites.

THE SUPERHERO
This stone figure from the palace of Sargon II at Dur-Sharrukin may represent Gilgamesh. The hero was famed for his great strength, which was a gift from his mother, the goddess Ninsun. His father was King Lugalbanda. Gilgamesh was said to be more god than man. His beauty came from the Sun god, Shamash, while his courage was a gift from Adad, the god of storms. The epic describes Gilgamesh as a cruel king. His people prayed for help and the gods sent Enkidu, the wild man. When Enkidu and Gilgamesh became friends, the gods sent monsters to kill them.

IMMORTAL STONES
This mound is the ruin of the ziggurat at Uruk. Parts of the city's walls still stand, too. The epic tells how Gilgamesh, who ruled the city, built those walls. After the king realized that he was mortal, and would die just as other humans did, he took consolation from Uruk. He understood that the splendor of the city would survive long after his death.

HUMBABA

This terrifying mask of clay represents the fire-breathing demon Humbaba (sometimes spelled Huwawa). He appears in the epic of Gilgamesh as the guardian of the Cedar Forest where the gods lived. Humbaba was slain by Gilgamesh and Enkidu, with the help of the Sun god Shamash and the Eight Winds. This face was made in Sippar in about 1700 BCE. Like many representations of Humbaba, it is modeled in the form of coiled animal intestines, like those used by priests for predicting the future.

Eyes were probably painted

Swallow

Dove

Raven

WINGED MESSENGERS

The epic of Gilgamesh offers the earliest account of the great flood that is also recorded in the Bible. Utnapishtim is the Mesopotamian version of Noah. The gods warn him of the flood so he builds an ark. Utnapishtim survives the flood for six days while humankind is destroyed. He releases a dove and a swallow but they return because they cannot find dry land. Then Utnapishtim releases a raven. It does not return, showing that the waters have receded.

Coils resemble intestines

Continuous coil is an omen of revolution

THE SERPENT

After Enkidu's death, Gilgamesh tried to find everlasting life. Utnapishtim, the only human to have become immortal, advised him to look for a magical plant called "The Old Man Grows Young." Gilgamesh found the plant on the seabed, but while he was sleeping, a snake stole and ate it. Since then, snakes have possessed the power to renew their skin by shedding it, but humans die because they lost the plant of everlasting youth.

Old skin is shed

NOAH'S ARK

In the Biblical account of the flood, the man who builds the ark is named Noah. God sends 40 days and nights of rain to destroy humankind and its wickedness, but spares Noah, who has lived a good life. The ark carries Noah, his family, and a pair of every kind of animal. After the flood, the ark comes to rest on Mount Ararat (in modern-day Turkey).

Bronze curved to wrap around gatepost

Scenes of people and horses decorate bands

Nail hammered into the metal

Assyrian knowledge

THE ASSYRIANS WERE RUTHLESS WARRIORS, but their empire (1120–612 BCE) brought stability to many lands. They were ready to learn from other cultures and to adopt traditions and customs different from their own. Ashurbanipal, who reigned from 668 to 627 BCE, prided himself as a linguist, mathematician, and writer. At least 10,000 cuneiform texts have been discovered at his royal libraries at Nineveh. The seventh century BCE was a great age of astronomical observation, arts and crafts, and musical notation. Assyrian scholarship was interwoven with superstition and myth, but it also contained early stirrings of scientific thought. The Assyrians were first-rate technicians, engineers, plumbers, and road builders. They quarried and transported great blocks of stone for their ambitious construction projects. They were also masters of irrigation. Eighteen canals were built to carry water to the city of Nineveh, and an impressive aqueduct has been found nearby at Jerwan.

PIVOTAL TECHNOLOGY

Decorative strips of bronze, about 10½ in (27 cm) high, were discovered between 1876 and 1956 at Balawat (ancient Imgur-Enlil), near the city of Nimrud. Dating from the reigns of Ashurnasirpal II and his son Shalmaneser III, the strips were identifed as bands that were once nailed to three pairs of massive wooden gates. Two belonged to Shalmaneser's summer palace, and the third to the temple. The gates were probably about 20 ft (6 m) high and 7½ ft (2.5 m) wide. They were not hinged, but attached to strong posts on pivots. Pushing the gate made the post turn on its pivot, allowing the gate to open.

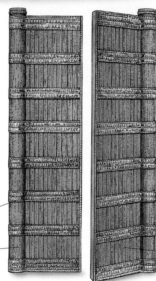

Bronze strip

Gatepost stands on a stone pivot beneath the floor

Gate is made of strong wood

Decapitated heads

Man holding scroll may be a war artist

Scribe holds hinged writing board

Soldier starts a bonfire

CARVED IN STONE

This Assyrian panel comes from the Southwest Palace at Nineveh and dates to around 645 BCE. More than 35 ft (10.5 m) high, it was carved from alabaster using copper and iron tools. It formed part of a story. The panel on the facing wall showed the conquest of peoples in southern Mesopotamia. In this panel, Assyrian scribes list the spoils of war. Archeologists have found writing boards like the one shown in this panel. They were covered in wax, which could be melted after use, so that the writing surface could be used more than once.

GLAZES AND GLASS

This colorful fragment of Assyrian glazed pottery shows a leaping mountain goat. Glazes are glossy or glassy surfaces created when clay is fired in kilns. They may have originally been discovered by accident, when grains of sand stuck to clay. During the Assyrian period, skilled craftworkers produced glazed pottery and bricks, as well as beautiful vessels of glass.

Sennacherib
surveys the scene

Worker uses
shaduf to scoop
river water

Teams of slaves
haul the sled with
thick reed ropes

Colossal bull statue
is transported on a
wooden sled

Laborers use a long
wooden lever to nudge
the sled forward

Quarry workers
carry baskets of
loose chippings

QUARRYING AND HAULAGE

Sennacherib, who ruled from 705 to 681 BCE, set up huge *lamassu* (winged bull) statues in his palace at Nineveh. This archeologist's drawing of a wall carving shows Sennacherib supervising the transit of a statue, protected by a detachment of armed guards. The massive block of stone, roughly shaped in the quarries, has been placed on a wooden sled. Too heavy to be carried by river, it is hauled overland using ropes, levers, and wooden rollers. The pulling power is provided by teams of slaves, no doubt captured during Assyria's many wars. Water for wetting the ropes and quenching the slaves' thirst is raised from the river by an ancient bucket system called a shaduf.

Cuneiform
script

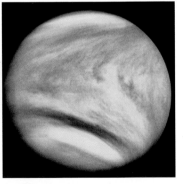

Pivot allows
pole to rise
and fall

THE SHADUF

Still used today by Egyptian farmers along the banks of the Nile, the shaduf is a mechanism for raising water that was invented in ancient Mesopotamia. It consists of a bucket or goatskin, used to hold the water, that is attached by rope to a pivoted pole. The pole has a counterbalance at the other end, which makes it easy to lift the bucket.

Broken
tablet is ¾ in
(22 mm) thick

OBSERVING THE HEAVENS

This clay tablet from the royal libraries in the palaces of Nineveh records observations of the planet Venus (above). It is an Assyrian copy, made in the seventh century BCE, of Babylonian data from around 1200 BCE during the reign of Ammisaduqa. Assyrian priests recorded movements of the Moon, Sun, planets, and stars. They were astrologers, believing that the fate of empires, rulers, and all humans was decided by signs in the heavens. These early stargazers are the fathers of the science of astronomy, thanks to their clear, detailed observations.

Babylon reborn

As one of Mesopotamia's wealthiest and most influential cities, Babylon had thrived in the age of Hammurabi, then fallen to the Assyrians. It rose to glory again under Nabopolassar, who founded a second Babylonian empire in 625 BCE. His son, Nebuchadnezzar II, defeated the Assyrians and Egyptians at the Battle of Carchemish in 605 BCE. He sacked Jerusalem in 586 BCE and forced many Jews into exile—the Babylonian captivity described in the Bible. Nebuchadnezzar also rebuilt Babylon's ziggurat and temple, and gave the city an impressive new wall. It was 11¼ miles (18 kilometers) long, and wide enough for a chariot to turn on its battlements!

MOTHER AND BABY
This small statue, modeled in terra-cotta, was made in the seventh century BCE. It shows a Babylonian mother feeding her baby and may have been placed in the home, to keep the household from harm. Most Mesopotamian statues portray gods and goddesses, mythical beasts, warfare, male rulers, or palace life. This image reminds us of the everyday lives of thousands of ordinary women in Babylon.

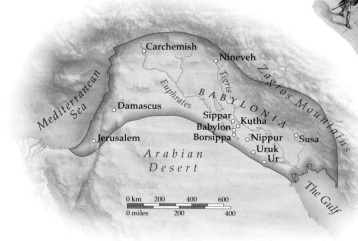

Simple bucket and pulley system draws water from wells up to the top level

An imaginary view of planted terraces

Steps over canal system lead up to the next terrace

THE NEW BABYLONIA
The second Babylonian Empire stretched from the borders of Egypt to the Zagros Mountains. Its power was shortlived, lasting less than a century. The empire was founded in 625 BCE by a commoner called Nabopolassar. His dynasty was overthrown in 555 BCE, and Nabonidus was made king. In 539 BCE Babylonia was defeated by the Persians at Opis, a city just north of Babylon.

Gate may have stood more than 48 ft (14 m)

Bricks have blue glaze

THE ISHTAR GATE
This is a reconstruction of one of eight gates leading into the inner city of Babylon. It was built in about 575 BCE and was dedicated to the goddess Ishtar. Through it passed the Processional Way, a sacred route to the temple of Marduk. The Ishtar Gate was faced with blue glazed bricks and decorated with designs of bulls and dragons.

Map labels:
Carchemish · Nineveh · Mediterranean Sea · Euphrates · Tigris · Zagros Mountains · BABYLONIA · Damascus · Sippar · Kutha · Babylon · Borsippa · Nippur · Susa · Jerusalem · Uruk · Ur · Arabian Desert · The Gulf

0 km 200 400 600
0 miles 200 400

Tumbling waterfall

Canals connected to wells feed the plants on the terraces

Well

Peaches

Pear

LILIES OF THE FIELD
The Babylonians used impressive irrigation methods to cultivate flowering plants and fruit trees in their dry and dusty land. They grew peach, pear, and pistachio nut trees as well as date palms. Shrubs included grapevines, grown for fruit, and native tamarisk, which provided a windbreak. Prized flowers included lilies and poppies. Poppies were grown for opium, which had been used as a drug and painkiller since Sumerian times.

Grapes

Poppy

Tamarisk

HANGING GARDENS
According to some ancient Greek writers, Babylon was famed for its terraced gardens, filled with exotic plants and watered by clever irrigation. They claimed that the Hanging Gardens were one of the Seven Wonders of the World, created by Nebuchadnezzar for his wife, Amytis. She was a Median princess who longed for the green countryside of her homeland. Some archeologists claim to have found likely sites, but so far no one has been able to prove that the gardens existed. There is no Babylonian account of them, either.

Lily

Rembrandt (working before the archeological rediscovery of Mesopotamia) paints God's warning in Hebrew script

Symbols of the gods: Moon (Sin), Sun (Shamash), Venus (Ishtar)

Nabonidus holds royal scepter

THE LAST KING
This pillar probably shows Nabonidus, who was chosen as king of Babylonia after the murder of the young king Labashi-Marduk in 556 BCE. Nabonidus was devoted to the god Sin. He went into exile in Arabia for some years, perhaps in response to an omen of ill fortune, while his son ruled as regent. Nabonidus was the last Babylonian king. In 539 BCE, he was defeated by the Persians, led by Cyrus the Great.

WRITING ON THE WALL
This masterpiece of about 1635 is by the Dutch painter Rembrandt. It portrays the Bible story of Belshazzar's Feast, at which wine was served in cups looted from the Jewish Temple in Jerusalem. Belshazzar (the son of Nabonidus) is warned by God that his days are numbered and that Babylon will fall to the Medes and Persians.

Onyx mace had a core of bronze

At the center of the world

NABOPOLASSAR MADE BABYLON THE POLITICAL CENTER of Mesopotamia again. It had long been regarded as the religious center, for the city was protected by the mighty god Marduk. Marduk had taken on the title of Bel ("lord") and become the most important of all the gods. His supremacy meant that Babylon was believed to be at the center of the universe. This idea was expressed in the creation epic *Enuma Elish* ("When on High"), a long poem written down in the 12th century BCE and sung as a hymn. It was recited by the high priest at Babylon's most important religious festival, the *Akitu*, which marked the Mesopotamian New Year. Held at the spring equinox, the *Akitu* was a 12-day public holiday, with plenty of music and singing. The Esagila, the temple of Marduk at Babylon, was at the center of the religious ceremonies. Here the king paid homage to Marduk. Statues of lesser gods, dressed in costly robes, were brought from other Mesopotamian cities by boat.

Salt Sea encircles the known world

Rectangle stands for Babylon

Euphrates flows down from the mountains

Long rectangle represents marshes

Circle stands for Susa

WORLD VIEW
This Babylonian clay tablet is a map of the Earth, with the northwest uppermost. The outer region is occupied by lands famed in Mesopotamian mythology. The circle represents the "Salt Sea" (the ocean that surrounds the world). The middle of the map shows the Euphrates River, flowing from its source in the Anatolian highlands. The cities of Babylon and Susa are located near the top and bottom of the river. The original of this map was made about 2,700 years ago.

SPRING BARLEY
The great Babylonian festival of *Akitu* began in the days of the Sumerian city-states, to mark the sowing of barley in the spring. From this original meaning, *Akitu* came to be a time for renewal and regeneration, of hopes for good fortune and abundant harvests in the coming year.

BABYLON THE MAGNIFICENT
Nebuchadnezzar's city was a spectacle of glazed bricks and colorful tiles. There were civic buildings, markets, workshops, courtyards, and more than 1,000 incense-filled temples. The Euphrates River brought merchants, travelers, and—during the *Akitu* festival—chanting priests bearing glittering statues of the gods. The *Akitu* parade left the temple of Marduk and headed along Babylon's Processional Way, passing Nebuchadnezzar's grand palace. It left the city through the Ishtar Gate and continued toward a rural temple.

Artist's vision of the Hanging Gardens

The Processional Way, a tiled road leading up to the Esagila

The Ishtar Gate

Scepter was found in many parts, and has been pieced together through guesswork

THE SCEPTER

At each *Akitu* festival, the king had to fetch his scepter or mace from the temple of Nabu (son of Marduk) at Borsippa and take it to the Esagila, the temple of Marduk at Babylon. Here, the king's scepter, his emblem of power, was taken away and the high priest struck the king across the face, in punishment for all his sins of the past year. Once the king had repented and been purified, his scepter was returned to him.

Etemenanki (ziggurat dedicated to Marduk)

BENEATH THE ZIGGURAT

This artist's impression captures Babylonian life in the shadow of the Etemenanki (see page 25), a ziggurat that may have been the model for the "Tower of Babel." The monument was enlarged with fired bricks during the reign of Nebuchadnezzar. The Jews, exiled here between 586 and 538 BCE, worshipped a single god and were contemptuous of Babylon's many gods and idols.

Nebuchadnezzar's palace was built around courtyards

Snake-dragon has two horns

Eyes were originally inlaid with precious stone

GOD'S DRAGON

This bronze snake-dragon or *mushhushshu* dates from the sixth century BCE. It would have fit on to the end of a pole and may have formed the head of a scepter, battle standard, or the central shaft of a chariot. Dragons like this decorated city walls and the Ishtar Gate. They were emblems of the god Marduk and recalled his defeat of the monstrous Tiamat, which had earned Marduk his superior role among the gods. Marduk's battle with Tiamat was depicted on the walls of the Esagila, Babylon's main temple.

SPRING FESTIVALS

Festivals like *Akitu* have been celebrated for thousands of years across western Asia. *Novruz, Nawruz,* or *Norouz* ("new day") is rooted in ancient Persian tradition with elements of the Zoroastrian faith and Islam. It is still a major festival, and is marked across the region, from Turkey to India. This *Norouz* feast table, decorated with painted eggs, is from Iran.

The Persians

WHILE BABYLON THRIVED during the age of Nebuchadnezzar, Mesopotamia's northern and eastern neighbors were becoming ever more powerful. Chief among them were the Medes and the Persians, ancestors of today's Kurds and Iranians. The Medes joined forces with the Babylonians to sack the Assyrian city of Nineveh in 612 BCE. Soon the Median Empire stretched from the Black Sea to Afghanistan. In about 550 BCE the Persian ruler Cyrus the Great rebelled against the Medes and founded the first Persian Empire, sometimes called the Achaemenid Empire. Cyrus defeated Babylonia in 539 BCE and crowned his son, Cambyses II, king of Babylonia. Cyrus was a wise ruler. He allowed Mesopotamia to play a key role in his new empire. All the same, Babylonia had lost its independence forever, and the Mesopotamians were beginning two centuries of life under Persian rule.

Short sword

Barsom (bundle of sticks used in religious ceremonies)

Spear was 7½ ft (2.25 m) long, with a gilded ball on its shaft if the soldier was of high rank

MEDIAN DRESS
This gold plaque from a temple shows a Mede wearing a hood, tunic, and pants. The Medes' language was closely related to that of the Persians. Both peoples were descended from groups of northern invaders who had arrived in Western Asia more than 500 years before. The Medes ruled the Persians until 550 BCE, when the tables were turned by Cyrus the Great.

THE FIRST PERSIAN EMPIRE
At its greatest extent the Achaemenid Empire stretched from Egypt and Thrace in the west, to Central Asia and India in the east. Darius I built a Royal Road, which ran 1,500 miles (2,500 km) from Susa to Sardis. He also divided the empire into regions called satrapies, one of which was Assyria-Babylonia. Each had its own governor, or satrap.

Archer wears a headband of twisted cord, a long, richly decorated tunic, and leather shoes

RUINS OF PERSEPOLIS
The Persian Empire had several capitals. The most splendid was Parsa, known to the Greeks as Persepolis. Founded by Darius I around 518 BCE, Persepolis had colonnaded halls and grand palaces. Excavation of its ruins, in modern Iran, began in the 1930s.

Headdress looks smooth, but would have been feathered

Scepter

CYRUS THE GREAT
King Cyrus, who reigned from around 590 to 529 BCE, overthrew Median rule and established Persian supremacy over all Western Asia. He was a great soldier but held his empire together with diplomacy rather than force. Cyrus was killed campaigning in the far north and was buried at his capital, Pasargadae.

Smooth, flared rim

DARIUS I
This wall carving from Persepolis shows Darius I, who reigned from 521 to 484 BCE. Darius appointed regional governors to run his empire and introduced a new tax system and gold coinage. He invaded Greece but was defeated at Marathon in 490 BCE.

Socket for an antler

Kneeling gazelle still shows signs of gilding

SOLDIERS OF THE GUARD
This mosaic of glazed brick is from the palace of Darius I at Susa, the former Elamite capital. It shows a parade of the crack troops of the royal bodyguard, known as the Immortals. Their numbers were always maintained at 10,000. Each soldier is dressed in fine robes and carries a spear and a bow with a quiver for his arrows. When fighting in battle, the Immortals may have worn more practical dress in the Median style.

SILVER FROM SUSA
This rhyton or drinking horn from the fifth century BCE was found at the palace of Darius at Susa. It is made of silver and was originally decorated with gold leaf. The handle is shaped like a gazelle. Animal designs were popular with Persian metalworkers, who created many treasures in silver.

The classical age

ALABASTER GODDESS
This small statue from about 250 BCE is decorated with gold and gemstones. The horns are in the Babylonian tradition, but the natural representation of the body is Hellenistic.

ALEXANDER THE GREAT
Born in 356 BCE, Alexander became one of the most brilliant generals the world has known. He was also skilled at dealing with the people he conquered across Asia. However, by the time of his death he was said to be often quarrelsome and drunk.

THE GREEKS NEVER FORGAVE THE PERSIANS for their invasions of the Greek homeland. In 334 BCE a Greek army, commanded by a young Macedonian ruler called Alexander, marched into Asia. He twice defeated the Persian king Darius III. Babylon, Susa, and Persepolis all opened their gates to the Greeks. Alexander planned to rebuild Mesopotamia but he died at Babylon in 323 BCE, aged just 33. Alexander's empire was divided between his generals. Seleucus I, former governor of Babylon, became its king in 305 BCE. He built a new capital at Seleucia, on the west bank of the Tigris. This grew into a city of 600,000 people, far greater than Babylon. In about 200 BCE the Greek rulers were ousted from Mesopotamia by the Parthians, a people from northeastern Persia. Meanwhile, a new power was on the rise in Europe— the Romans. Roman and Parthian armies fought each other endlessly, and Mesopotamia was their battlegound. Seleucia was finally destroyed in 164 CE. In 227 CE a new Persian dynasty gained control of the region. Known as the Sassanids, they held on to power until 636 CE.

ALEXANDER'S CONQUESTS
Alexander the Great created a vast new territory out of the ruins of the Persian Empire. It extended from Egypt to the Indus River. On his death these lands were shared out among his followers. The Anatagonid dynasty ruled in Macedonia, the Ptolemies in Egypt, and the Seleucids in Asia, but these Hellenistic kingdoms eventually fell to the Romans and Parthians.

Hercules holds up the defeated boar

King cowers in bronze jar

GREECE AND ASIA
This vase shows a scene from Greek mythology, in which the god Hercules defeats a wild boar. The Greeks had always interacted with Asian culture, and this was especially true after Alexander's conquest. By the time of Seleucid rule, Hercules and the Mesopotamian god Nergal were seen as one and the same. Later, Hercules was associated with the Persian warrior god, Verethragna.

Frontal pose is typical of Parthian sculpture

A ROYAL PARTHIAN
This statue comes from Hatra (modern Al-Hadr, in Iraq). Hatra was a Seleucid city that came under Parthian control but kept Greek as its language and on its coins. The city was a melting pot for an extraordinary mixture of cultures. All sorts of gods were worshiped alongside one another, in the Mesopotamian, Greek, and Persian traditions. This statue reflects the same mix of cultural influences. It represents Prince Abd Samya, who lived in the first century BCE. His father, King Sanatruces, restored order in troubled times.

Prince raises hand in greeting

Tunic has fitted sleeves

THE PARTHIAN SHOT
Parthian mounted archers were famous for being able to shoot arrows backward with great accuracy while galloping at high speed. They fought alongside an effective heavy cavalry. With their superior speed and mobility, the Parthians were able to prevent the mighty Roman army from advancing beyond the banks of the Euphrates, although the two sides clashed for 270 years.

Palm frond's significance is not known

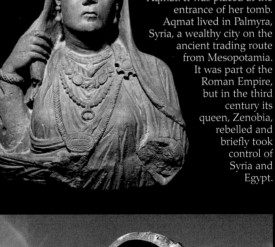

A SYRIAN LADY
This Roman-style statue, from the second century CE, shows a woman named Aqmat. It was placed at the entrance of her tomb. Aqmat lived in Palmyra, Syria, a wealthy city on the ancient trading route from Mesopotamia. It was part of the Roman Empire, but in the third century its queen, Zenobia, rebelled and briefly took control of Syria and Egypt.

Appliqué decoration shows the guardian goddess, Athena-Allat

Buckled belt draws in the tunic at the waist

The Greek messenger god, Hermes, with his staff

LANDMARK IN CTESIPHON
Ctesiphon was built on the site of Opis, opposite Seleucia on the Tigris River. It was the chief city of the Parthians and was repeatedly attacked by Rome. When the Persian Sassanids ruled Mesopotamia, it became the site of a fabulous palace built by Chosroes I, who ruled from 531 to 579 CE. A magnificent arch survives on the site to this day.

Leggings protected against chafing when on horseback

The Islamic age

Bilal (crescent moon), symbol of Islam

IN THE ARABIAN DESERT a new religion called Islam was firing people with enthusiasm. Its followers pledged submission to one God, whose messenger Muhammad had lived from 570 to 632 CE. Under the leadership of rulers called caliphs, Arab armies spread the faith across Asia and North Africa. They defeated the Persians at Qadisiyah in 637, pulled down Ctesiphon, and used its stones to build a dazzling new capital on the Tigris in 762. Founded by Caliph Al-Mansur, the city was called Medinat as-Salaam ("city of peace") or Baghdad. It was almost 2 miles (3 kilometers) across and had three rings of walls. Under Arab, Persian, and Turkic influences, Mesopotamia prospered once more as a center of trade, architecture, art, poetry, music, medicine, and astronomy.

MOSUL METALWORK
This marvelous pitcher was made in the city of Mosul in 1232. Its decorations feature scenes from court life, including a horseman, a pet cheetah, a hunting scene, a lady riding a camel, and another lady with her jewels. Some of the scenes are from the *Shahnama* ("Book of Kings"), a masterpiece written by the great Persian poet Firdawsi (c. 935–1020).

Brass inlaid with silver and copper

HARUN AL-RASHID
This illuminated manuscript shows Caliph Harun Al-Rashid, sitting in judgment. Baghdad flourished during his reign (786–809 CE). Merchants made the city wealthy and artists made it splendid. Harun created a court famed for its luxury, depicted in the tales of *A Thousand and One Nights*.

Musicians with harp and lute

Courtier on horseback

Triangular sail called a lateen

THE ABBASID CALIPHATE
In the eighth century CE Baghdad became the capital of the Abbasid caliphate, the most powerful state in the Muslim world. Its Islamic rulers, the caliphs, claimed descent from Abbas, the uncle of Muhammad. They ruled a vast territory, from Mecca (Muhammad's birthplace) to Central Asia. Major Mesopotamian cities included Basra in the south and Mosul in the north. Abbasid power declined after 945.

SEAFARERS AND MERCHANTS
Muslim merchants sailed across the Indian Ocean, using the monsoon winds, in wooden ships called dhows. They traded in India, Southeast Asia, and down the coasts of east Africa. This was the world made legendary in the tales of Sinbad the Sailor.

A CALL TO PRAYER

This is a minaret, a tower from which Muslims are called to prayer. It was built in 859 CE, in the Abbasid period, and is part of the Abu-Dulaf mosque in Samarra. It is 112 ft (34 m) high and its spiral access gives it a layered appearance rather like the ancient ziggurats. Samarra was a new city founded in 833 to the north of Baghdad. It became renowned as a center of architecture, arts, and crafts.

SOUND THE TRUMPETS!

The detail below is from a manuscript of Al-Hariri's *Maqamat* ("Meetings"), made in Baghdad in 1237. It shows the caliph's trumpeters and standard-bearers signaling the end of Ramadan, the Islamic month of fasting. Islam has five "pillars" or duties—confession of faith, prayer five times daily, almsgiving, fasting, and pilgrimage. Two rival traditions arose within the faith: Sunni or orthodox Islam, and Shi'a. They differ in their original allegiance to Muhammad's successors. Sunni Islam emphasizes the Islamic community's role of safeguarding Muhammad's teachings, while Shi'a focuses on the interpretive role of spiritual leaders called imams.

Timur is shown in a central Asian-style tent called a yurt

Calligraphy flourished under Islam

Courtly dancers and musicians

Bold colors preserved on vellum

IN LATER HISTORY

The later Middle Ages saw waves of invaders pour into Mesopotamia from Central Asia. Seljuk Turks took effective control of Baghdad in 1055. Mongol horsemen devastated Mesopotamia in 1229 and returned to Baghdad in 1258. This 16th-century miniature shows the military leader Timur (also known as Tamburlaine), a Mongol and Muslim, whose soldiers destroyed many of the region's irrigation canals in 1401. After a further period of Persian rule, Mesopotamia became a backwater of the Turkish Ottoman Empire. Rule from the Ottoman capital, Istanbul (previously Constantinople), lasted from 1534 to 1918. Most of Mesopotamia then became the modern nation of Iraq. Vast oil reserves were discovered, but the political situation was unstable and often violent. Powerful outsiders, European and American, repeatedly intervened in Iraqi affairs. Iraq's future remains uncertain today—but the resilience and endurance of the peoples in this region is proven by history.

Uncovering the past

FASHION STATEMENT
This painting shows Enid, wife of archeologist A. H. Layard, who had excavated Nimrud (Kalhu). In 1869, Layard gave his young bride jewelry made of cylinder seals. Such objects became the height of fashion, as Mesopotamian treasures went on display in European museums for the first time.

OVER MANY CENTURIES brick turned to dust, wind eroded the ziggurats, sandstorms buried palaces. The treasures of the Mesopotamians lay hidden in the desert. However, all was not lost. In the 19th century, foreign scholars and adventurers began to visit ancient Mesopotamia. Some were fascinated by examples of the mysterious cuneiform script, others by stories from the Bible. As precious objects were unearthed, many fabulous discoveries were shipped off to museums in Europe and the US. Soon Mesopotamians (later, Iraqis) began to take pride in studying their ancient history. The 20th century saw scientific excavations in the region, aided by technological inventions such as radioactive dating methods. In the early 21st century, this archeological progress suffered a severe setback. The Iraq War in 2003 led to the looting of treasures from the Iraq Museum in Baghdad, widespread damage to ancient sites, and the exile of leading Mesopotamian scholars.

SITE OF THE DIG
Each archeological site must be carefully surveyed, excavated, measured, and photographed. The work requires hard physical labor as well as endless patience, often in dusty conditions and great heat. The dig here took place in 2001 at the Sumerian site of Umma, in southern Iraq. It was led by the Iraqi archeologist Nawala al-Mutawalli. She went there to catalog the site and to secure it against looters.

PIONEERS OF ARCHEOLOGY
In this illustration A. H. Layard is showing off one of his Assyrian finds. He was one of many archeologists who excavated in Mesopotamia in the 19th century. Others included Henry Rawlinson and Paul Emile Botta in the 1840s, Hormuzd Rassam from the 1850s onward, and Ernest de Sarzec and Robert Koldewey in the 1880s.

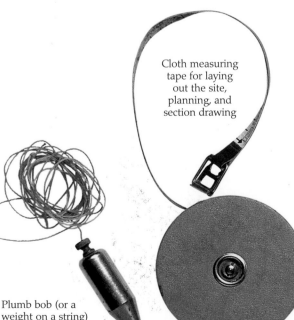

Cloth measuring tape for laying out the site, planning, and section drawing

Plumb bob (or a weight on a string) for plotting straight vertical lines

Handpick for digging around an artifact

THE TRENCH
These archeologists are examining a plan of a trench. After a trench has been dug it is drawn to scale, so that archeologists can record the precise position of any finds. This is important, because each period of settlement in a city leaves its own layer of remains. Each layer may be dated by finds such as pottery, tools, or clay tablets.

PRECIOUS FINDS
Every object discovered on a dig must be carefully removed and identified. It must also be kept secure from thieves. This photograph shows armed looters attacking the site of Ishan Bakhriyat in 2003. They stole whatever they could carry off, and many years' worth of systematic archeological research were undone.

TOOLS OF THE TRADE
Many of the archeologist's tools are fairly basic. They include picks, shovels, brushes, trowels, sieves, measuring poles, and cameras. All finds must be painstakingly cleaned, packed, and cataloged. Away from the site, high technology plays its part. Laboratory technicians take X-ray images, analyze plant or animal remains, and date finds by measuring the radioactive materials they naturally contain—a technique called radiocarbon dating.

CONSERVATION AND RESTORATION QUESTIONS
In the conservation laboratory of the Iraq Museum in Baghdad, archeologist Zainab Bahrani oversees restoration of a lion statue from around 1800 BCE. It was damaged during looting at the start of the Iraq War. The team is re-laying the terra-cotta shards of "fur" over a new plaster core. The goals of conservation (keeping and caring for objects) and restoration (repairing or recreating) can sometimes be at odds and pose problems for archeologists. How far should they go? What methods should they use?

Hole was for threading a string handle

Fired clay has been painted red

Deer beside stylized tree

REVEALED
This urn comes from Khafaji, near Baghdad, and dates from 2700 BCE. Once an object like this has been dug up, cleaned, and pieced together, it can finally go on display in a museum or gallery. No photograph has the same impact as the real object, made by skilled hands thousands of years ago.

Pointing trowel for digging and scraping

Brush for gently cleaning away grains of loose soil

Dental picks for fine work or fragile remains

Photo scale for showing an object's size when photographed

5Cm

Timeline of Mesopotamia

BECAUSE THE WORLD'S FIRST CIVILIZATIONS arose in Mesopotamia, the length of its recorded history is without parallel. During the last 11 millennia many different peoples have lived around the Tigris and Euphrates rivers, or ruled the cities of the region. The history of these peoples is complicated, but it is remarkable how much continuity exists, as each new age adopted ideas and customs from its predecessors.

A 19th-century drawing of Mesopotamian cylinder seals

Sumerian clay tablet from c. 2050 BCE, with accounts written in cuneiform script

BCE (Before Common Era)

C. 70000 EARLY PEOPLE
Neanderthal hunter-gatherers live in caves in northern Mesopotamia.

C. 35000 MODERN HUMANS
In the Upper Palaeolithic (Old Stone Age) period, modern humans (*Homo sapiens*) use improved stone tools and weapons.

C. 9500 THE FIRST FARMERS
Domestication (farming) of animals and crops in the Fertile Crescent. Early artists make clay figurines and carved bone work. Weapons have tips of obsidian, imported from Anatolia.

C. 7000–4000 VILLAGE SETTLEMENTS
Increased settlement in Mesopotamia. Villages grow and people make advances in irrigation, pottery, and copper pots and weapons.

C. 4000 GROWTH OF TOWNS
Society becomes divided into social classes. Religious shrines and temples are built. Mud bricks are manufactured. Towns develop, such as Uruk in southern Mesopotamia.

C. 3500 SUMERIAN CITY-STATES
Independent states form in Sumer (southern Mesopotamia) centered around cities and temples. Important city-states include Eridu, Uruk, Kish, Ur, Nippur, and Lagash. There is constant warfare between them.

C. 3500–3000 AGE OF INVENTIONS
New technologies include the world's first wheeled vehicles, the potter's wheel, and the manufacture of bronze. Writing is invented, in the form of wedge-shaped (cuneiform) symbols. The first cylinder seals are made.

C. 2800 THE GREAT FLOOD
Possible date for one of several periods of severe flooding across western Asia, an event made into legend in the epic of Gilgamesh.

C. 2750 THE RISE OF UR
Kings rule Ur, and their tombs contain many treasures in gold and lapis lazuli. Trade with the Gulf, Arabia, Afghanistan, and the Indus Valley.

C. 2700 THE AGE OF GILGAMESH
Gilgamesh is said to have ruled Uruk. Legends about him are written down from c. 2000.

C. 2525 CITY-STATES AT WAR
Bitter war between Lagash and Umma.

C. 2350 THE EARLIEST LIBRARY
Court officials in Ebla, northern Syria, archive more than 20,000 clay tablets, recording diplomatic contacts and trade. Some are in Sumerian script, showing that Ebla had links with southern Mesopotamia.

2334 THE AKKADIAN EMPIRE
Sargon of Akkad rules, conquering the Sumerian city-states and founding the world's first empire.

2254–2218 REIGN OF NARAM-SIN
Naram-Sin's rule marks the high point of Akkadian power.

2112–2095 UR REGAINS POWER
The reign of Ur-Nammu and a return to power of the Sumerian city-states. Ur-Nammu builds several ziggurats.

2080–2060 GUDEA OF LAGASH
King Gudea, a great builder of temples, rules from Lagash.

Copper peg from the foundations of the temple at ancient Girsu, showing King Gudea of Lagash

C. 2000 THE RISE OF ASHUR
The Assyrian city of Ashur grows wealthy from trade with Anatolia (modern Turkey).

1900 AMORITES TAKE BABYLON
A nomadic desert people, the Amurru or Amorites, win control of the city of Babylon.

1792 HAMMURABI'S REIGN BEGINS
Hammurabi, born in about 1810, becomes the sixth ruler of Babylon, beginning a 42-year reign and founding the first Babylonian empire.

1787 ISIN DEFEATED
The southern city-state of Isin (modern Ishan Bakhriyat) is defeated by Hammurabi.

1763–1761 BABYLON EXPANDS
Hammurabi conquers the city-states of Larsa, Mari, Eshnunna, and perhaps Ashur, expanding the first Babylonian empire far northward along the Tigris and Euphrates rivers.

1760 HAMMURABI'S LAWS
Hammurabi makes public the laws of Babylonia, engraving them on an upright stone pillar or stele. This is one of the world's earliest legal codes.

C. 1650 RISE OF THE HITTITES
The Hittites become powerful in Anatolia. Labarnas I founds a dynasty in Kussara. His son Labarnas II moves the Hittite capital to Hattusas.

1595 HITTITES ATTACK BABYLON
The Hittite king, Mursilis, marches south from the Taurus Mountains to sack the city of Babylon.

C. 1480 KINGDOM OF MITTANI
The Hurrian kingdom of Mittani, a union of smaller states, reaches the height of its power in the north.

C. 1450 KASSITE CONTROL
The Kassites occupy southern Mesopotamia and, until 1154, rule Babylon.

1274 BATTLE OF QADESH
The expanding Egyptian and Hittite empires clash at Qadesh. There is no clear winner.

C. 1200–900 DARK AGE
A period of political unrest and social disruption, possibly brought about by an increasingly dry climate.

1120 RISE OF ASSYRIAN POWER
Tiglath-pileser I founds a new Assyrian empire.

Stone relief from c. 645 BCE, showing Assyrian soldiers using slingshots

C. 1000–911 ASSYRIAN SETBACK
The Assyrian Empire comes under attack from Aramaeans and other peoples who settle in Mesopotamia. Spread of the Aramaic language.

883–612 AGE OF PALACES
Assyrian Empire expands across western Asia into Egypt. Palaces are built at Nimrud (ancient Kalhu), Dur-Sharrukin (Khorsabad), and Nineveh. After the death of Ashurbanipal in 631, Assyrian power declines.

626–539 SECOND BABYLONIAN EMPIRE
Babylon returns to power under Nabopolassar. An alliance of Medes and Babylonians destroys Nineveh in 612.

605 NEBUCHADNEZZAR'S VICTORIES
Nebuchadnezzar II defeats Assyrians and Egyptians at Carchemish. He sacks Jerusalem in 586, exiling many Jews to Babylon (a time Biblical scholars call the Babylonian Captivity).

C. 575 THE ISHTAR GATE
Nebuchadnezzar II rebuilds Babylon.

Part of the decoration of Babylon's Ishtar Gate (c. 575 BCE), showing a bull

539 PERSIA DEFEATS BABYLONIA
The Persian king Cyrus the Great takes the city of Babylon. Mesopotamia becomes a part of the mighty Persian Empire.

518 PERSEPOLIS
Darius I builds the great palace at Persepolis.

334 ALEXANDER INVADES
Macedonian king Alexander the Great leads a Greek army into Asia and defeats Darius III of Persia. He conquers lands from Greece to India.

323 ALEXANDER DIES
Alexander dies in Babylon, seven years after his army first entered the city.

305 SELEUCID DYNASTY
Seleucis I "Nicator" founds Greek dynasty, building a new capital at Seleucia. Spread of Hellenistic (Greek) culture in Asia.

C. 200 PARTHIAN POWER
The Parthians, from the northeast of Persia, end Seleucid power in Mesopotamia. Their new capital is Ctesiphon.

CE (COMMON ERA)

75 CUNEIFORM SCRIPT IN DECLINE
The last known use of cuneiform script.

117 ROMAN MESOPOTAMIA
Between 115 and 117 the Roman Empire acquires Mesopotamia and Assyria, but it never manages to maintain permanent control.

164 END OF SELEUCIA
The city is finally destroyed, during the long Roman-Parthian wars.

227 PERSIA REGAINS POWER
Persian rule is reestablished in Mesopotamia under the Sassanid dynasty.

241 HATRA DESTROYED
The city of Hatra is destroyed by the Sassanid Persian ruler, Shapur I.

531–579 CHOSROES I REIGNS
The Persian ruler Chosroes builds at Ctesiphon.

600 CHRISTIAN MESOPOTAMIA
Many Mesopotamians are by now followers of the Christian faith.

637 WARRIORS OF ISLAM
Arabs defeat the Persians at Qadisiyah, bringing the new faith of Islam to the region.

762 NEW ABBASID CAPITAL
Caliph Al-Mansur founds Baghdad, known as Medinat as-Salaam ("city of peace").

786-809 HARUN AL-RASHID
Reign of Harun Al-Rashid in Baghdad, the golden age of the Abbasid caliphate.

1055 SELJUK TURKS
Baghdad is captured as Seljuk Turks extend their power across the Middle East.

1229 AND 1258 MONGOL INVASION
Hundreds of thousands slaughtered in Baghdad by invading Mongol armies.

1401 CANALS AND FIELDS DESTROYED
Mesopotamia is laid waste by the Mongol and Turkic followers of the warlord Timur.

1534–1918 OTTOMAN EMPIRE
Mesopotamia is ruled from Istanbul, as part of the Ottoman Empire.

1920–1932 BRITISH MANDATE
Britain is mandated (commissioned) to govern Iraq by the League of Nations.

1932 INDEPENDENT IRAQ
The nation of Iraq is formed.

2003 ARCHEOLOGICAL SITES AT RISK
Widespread looting following US-led invasion.

Sculpted head of Alexander the Great

A to Z of famous people

HISTORICAL FIGURES

Stele showing the Assyrian king Ashurbanipal carrying a basket of clay on his head

ALEXANDER THE GREAT (356–323 BCE)
Macedonian king Alexander led a Greek army into Asia, defeated the first Persian empire, and founded a new empire that included all Mesopotamia. He died at Babylon.

ASHURBANIPAL (REIGNED 668–627 BCE)
The last great Assyrian king, Ashurbanipal ruled in Nineveh from around 669 BCE and established a remarkable library. His empire stretched from Elam in the east to Egypt.

ASHURNASIRPAL II (R. 883–859 BCE)
A ruthless military leader, Ashurnasirpal II pushed the borders of the Assyrian Empire west to Lebanon. In 879 BCE he moved the capital to Nimrud, where he built the Northwest Palace.

CHOSROES I (R. 531–579 CE)
Sassanid king of Persia, Chosroes (or Khosrau) fought the Byzantine Empire for years. He built many fine palaces, including one in the old Parthian capital of Ctesiphon.

CYRUS THE GREAT (R. 590–529 BCE)
Cyrus (or Kourosh) overthrew Median rule to found the first Persian Empire. He defeated Babylonia in 539 BCE and made his son, Cambyses II, king of Babylonia.

ENHEDUANNA (C. 2250 BCE)
The first named author in history, Enheduanna was the daughter of King Sargon of Akkad. He appointed her to be high priestess of the Moon god, Nanna, in Ur.

GILGAMESH (C. 2650 BCE)
The legendary fifth king of Uruk, Gilgamesh came to be seen as a semidivine superhero. His epic exploits were written down over a period of thousands of years.

HAMMURABI (R. 1792–1750 BCE)
Hammurabi came to the throne of Babylon in 1792 BCE. He founded the first Babylonian empire and is remembered for his extensive legal code, one of the earliest to survive.

HARUN AL-RASHID (C. 763–809 CE)
The most famous of all Abbasid caliphs, Harun ruled from Baghdad from 786 CE. He presided over an age of trade, scholarship, and great artistic achievement.

NABONIDUS (R. 555–539 CE)
A commoner, Nabonidus became king of Babylon in 555 CE. He spent 10 years exiled in Arabia while his son Belshazzar ruled in his place. Nabonidus returned in 539 CE, but his kingdom fell to the Persians the same year.

NABOPOLASSAR (R. 626–605 BCE)
After allying himself with the Medes, Nabopolassar of Babylon sacked Nineveh in 612 BCE. He overthrew Assyrian power and founded the second Babylonian empire.

NARAM-SIN (R. 2254–2218 BCE)
The grandson of Sargon of Akkad, Naram-Sin was a warrior and the most powerful ruler of the Akkadian Empire. He claimed to be a god.

Diorite sculpture of a king, possibly Hammurabi

King Nebuchadnezzar II, who ruled Babylon from 604 BCE and rebuilt the city

NEBUCHADNEZZAR II (R. 604–562 BCE)
A Babylonian ruler, Nebuchadnezzar defeated the Assyrians and Egyptians in 605 BCE and sacked Jeruslaem in 586 BCE.

PUABI (C. 2600 BCE)
Puabi was queen or high priestess in Ur. Little is known of her life, but her grave was one of the richest at Ur.

SARGON (R. 2334–2279 BCE)
Sargon (or Sharrum-Kin) founded the world's first empire, Akkad. Its influence overwhelmed Sumer and spread as far as the Mediterranean.

SARGON II (R. 722–705 BCE)
Naming himself after the founder of the Akkadian Empire, Sargon II seized the Assyrian throne in 722 BCE. He built a palace at Dur-Sharrukin (modern Khorsabad).

SELEUCUS I (C. 358–281 BCE)
Greek governor of Babylonia under Alexander the Great, Seleucus founded a Hellenistic Asian empire and built the city of Seleucia.

SENNACHERIB (R. 704–681 BCE)
Assyrian king Sennacherib rebuilt the city of Nineveh on a grand scale around 700 BCE.

TIGLATH-PILESER III (R. 744–727 BCE)
A king and a military leader, Tiglath-pileser III (or Pulu) greatly expanded Assyrian rule.

UR-NAMMU (R. 2112–2095 BCE)
Founder of the third ruling dynasty of Ur, King Ur-Nammu came to rule a large area of Sumer after the collapse of the Akkadian Empire. He built ziggurats at Ur, Eridu, Nippur, and Uruk.

ZENOBIA (R. 262–272 CE)
An Arab queen of Palmyra, in Syria, Zenobia conquered Egypt and large areas of western Asia before the Romans defeated her.

ARCHEOLOGISTS AND SCHOLARS

BAQIR, TAHA (1912–1984)
Iraqi archeologist Baqir excavated Tall Harmal (the ancient city of Shaduppum) and discovered early legal codes. He was curator of the Iraq Museum in Baghdad (1941–1953) and Director General of Iraqi Antiquities (1958–1963).

BELL, GERTRUDE (1868–1926)
A British official in Mesopotamia at the end of World War I, Bell became the first Director of Antiquities for Iraq. She left money to fund the British School of Archeology in Iraq.

BOTTA, PAUL-EMILE (1802–1870)
Botta excavated Dur-Sharrukin (Khorsabad) and Nineveh in 1842–1843, believing the former to be the latter. A French diplomat, he shipped many Assyrian sculptures back to Paris.

CHRISTIE, AGATHA (1890–1976)
This famous English crime writer visited Ur in 1925, where she met her future husband, Max Mallowan. In 1936 she wrote *Murder in Mesopotamia*, a thriller set on a dig in Iraq.

CRESWELL, K. A. C. (1879–1974)
An expert on Islamic architecture, Creswell toured the Middle East extensively, recording its monuments in words and photographs. He left his archives to the Ashmolean Museum, Oxford.

GEORGE, ANDREW (B. 1955)
Professor at the School of Oriental and African Studies in London, George is an expert in the language of Babylonia and has made a classic translation of the text of the epic of Gilgamesh.

GEORGE, DONNY (B. 1950)
A leading expert on Mesopotamia, George was an important figure in the Iraq Museum, Baghdad, during the crises and wars of 1990 to 2003. In 2006, as growing violence threatened antiquities, he resigned as director of Iraq's State Board of Antiquities and Heritage.

Watercolor portrait of Sir Austen Henry Layard

Professor Donny George at the British Museum

JACOBSEN, THORKILD (1904–1993)
Danish-born Jacobsen was a greatly respected American scholar who studied ancient Sumerian texts, including poetry and the king lists. With Seton Lloyd he discovered the Assyrian aqueduct built by Sennacherib.

KOLDEWEY, ROBERT (1855–1925)
German archeologist Koldewey excavated the Ishtar Gate, Processional Way, temples, palace, and ziggurat at Babylon. He mistakenly thought he had also found the Hanging Gardens.

KRAMER, SAMUEL NOAH (1897–1990)
Born in Ukraine, Kramer was raised in the United States, where he became a world expert in Sumerian history and language.

LAYARD, AUSTEN HENRY (1817–1894)
British archeologist A. H. Layard excavated Nimrud and identified the true site of Nineveh. He sent back many statues and tablets to the British Museum in London.

LLOYD, SETON (1902–1996)
This English archeologist trained the first generation of Iraqi archeologists. He helped to found the Iraq Museum in Baghdad and also carried out excavations at Eridu.

MAHMOUD, MUZAHIM (B. 1947)
Between 1988 and 1992, this Iraqi archeologist discovered four tombs packed with gold treasure at Ashurnasipal II's palace at Nimrud.

MALLOWAN, MAX (1904–1978)
A student of Leonard Woolley's, Mallowan carried out excavations at Ur, Nimrud, and Nineveh from the 1920s to the 1950s. He was married to the writer Agatha Christie.

NEUGEBAUER, OTTO (1899–1990)
Austrian-American Neugebauer was a math historian who learned Akkadian, investigated Babylonian mathematics and astronomy, and revealed how advanced they were.

PARROT, ANDRÉ (1901–1980)
French archeologist Parrot excavated Mari, in Syria, from 1933 to 1974. He wrote classic books on Sumer, Mari, and Ashur, and was director of the Louvre Museum in Paris from 1968 to 1972.

PLACE, VICTOR (1818–1875)
This famous French archeologist excavated Khorsabad between 1852 and 1855, and took artifacts from Nineveh to the Louvre in Paris.

RASSAM, HORMUZD (1826–1910)
An Assyrian archeologist, born in Mosul, Rassam was an assistant to A. H. Layard before excavating at Nimrud and Nineveh. His most important discovery was the Balawat Gates.

RAWLINSON, HENRY (1810–1895)
A British soldier and diplomat, Rawlinson spent many years in Mesopotamia. He pioneered the study and decipherment of the cuneiform script.

REINER, ERICA (1924–2005)
A brilliant American scholar based at Chicago's Oriental Institute, Reiner compiled the first comprehensive dictionary of the Akkadian language. She also studied Babylonian science, including medicine and astronomy.

SAFAR, FUAD (DIED 1978)
This eminent Iraqi archeologist excavated many sites including Tell Hassuna, Eridu, Hatra, and the early Islamic site of Wasit.

SARZAC, ERNEST DE (1832–1901)
This French archeologist was the first to discover the sites of Sumer, excavating at Telloh (ancient Girsu) in 1877–1878 and 1880–1881.

SMITH, GEORGE (1840–1876)
Smith's translations of cuneiform led to new insights into the Bible. He later excavated at Nineveh, but died of a fever in Syria.

WOOLLEY, LEONARD (1880–1960)
English archeologist Woolley excavated at Carchemish and most notably at Ur in the 1920s and '30s, where he uncovered the Royal Tombs.

Leonard Woolley during excavations at Ur

A to Z of ancient sites

Eroded ziggurats and mounds blend into dusty, arid landscapes. Today it is hard to imagine ancient Mesopotamian cities as they were in their days of splendor. Yet for 200 years these sites have provided archeologists with fascinating glimpses of the world's first civilizations. The soil still contains precious remains, but in recent years warfare and lawlessness have damaged or put at risk many Iraqi sites. Securing and conserving them is a major task for the future.

Artist's impression of Babylon's fabled Hanging Gardens

ASHUR (QAL'AT SHERQAT)
Also known as Assur, this ancient city gave its name to Assyria. It is located about 60 miles (100 km) south of Mosul in Iraq and occupies a rocky outcrop on the west bank of the Tigris River. Ashur was occupied from the middle of the third millennium BCE and was the Assyrian capital from the 14th to the ninth century BCE. It was destroyed by the Medes and Babylonians in 614 BCE, but resettled by the Parthians in the first and second centuries CE. Between 1903 and 1913 German archeologists uncovered temples here, the Old Palace, and some 16,000 cuneiform tablets.

The ziggurat at Dur Untash (Choga Zanbil)

BABYLON
Ancient Babylon stood on the Euphrates River. It was founded in the third millennium BCE and had two great periods of power, first under Hammurabi (r. 1792–1750 BCE) and then in the seventh and sixth centuries BCE. Today's ruins, which lie 56 miles (90 km) south of Baghdad, the Iraqi capital, date mostly from the latter period. The remains include three mounds and ramparts. Excavations by Robert Koldewey between 1899 and 1917 revealed remains of the city's great ziggurat and the Ishtar Gate. Koldewey also believed that he had discovered the Hanging Gardens of Babylon, one of the Seven Wonders of the World described by the Greek writer Philo of Byzantium. Inappropriate "restorations" were carried out at the site in the 1990s by Iraqi dictator Saddam Hussein. A US military camp and helicopter landing pad was located on the site in the Iraq War of 2003, and a British Museum investigation reported substantial damage.

DUR-SHARRUKIN (KHORSABAD)
The village of Khorsabad lies 13 miles (20 km) northeast of Mosul in Iraq. It was the site of Dur-Sharrukin, a new Assyrian capital commenced by Sargon II in 713 BCE. He moved his court there in 706 BCE, before work was quite completed, but died the following year and the site was abandoned. Sargon's palace was excavated by Paul-Emile Botta and Victor Place in the 19th century and by the Oriental Institute of Chicago from 1928 to 1935.

DUR UNTASH (CHOGA ZANBIL)
Founded in about 1250 BCE, Dur Untash was the holy city of the Elamite kingdom. It was built 25 miles (40 km) to the south of Susa in what is now southwestern Iran. Despite being ringed by three massive walls, the city was destroyed by the Assyrian king Ashurbanipal in 640 BCE. Even so, it remains an impressive site. It has the best preserved of all the ancient ziggurats, still standing at about half of its original height. It has been a UNESCO World Heritage Site since 1979.

ERIDU (ABU SHAHRAIN)
Abu Shahrain is in southern Iraq, about 200 miles (315 km) southeast of Baghdad. It is the site of Eridu, one of the earliest Sumerian cities. The site, just 7 miles (11 km) southwest of Ur, was excavated in the 1940s by Fuad Safar and Seton Lloyd. Its importance lies in its successive temples. There is a large palace of the third millennium BCE and remains of a ziggurat raised by Ur-Nammu in about 2100 BCE. Some modern scholars have suggested that Eridu, not Babylon, was the city of Babel mentioned in the Bible, and that its ziggurat was the original Tower of Babel.

Tribute-bearers carved in stone at Persepolis

"Ram Caught in the Thicket," an artifact from Ur

HATRA (AL-HADR)
This site is 70 miles (110 km) southwest of Mosul, in Iraq, on the edge of the desert. It was a fortified city on the Parthian frontier, where many cultures mingled. It was at the forefront of battles with the Roman Empire in the second century CE. A UNESCO World Heritage Site since 1985, it includes defensive towers and ancient temples.

KALHU (TELL NIMRUD)
This site is 24 miles (38 km) southeast of Mosul, in modern Iraq. It was repeatedly excavated in the 19th and 20th centuries. At first it was believed to be the site of Nineveh, and later became known as Nimrud. Kalhu was the Assyrian capital from about 884 to 710 BCE. It was destroyed in 612 BCE. The site includes the remains of several palaces and temples and has yielded a wealth of gold, statues and monuments, and cuneiform tablets.

MARI (TELL HARIRI)
Ancient Mari lies on the west bank of the Euphrates River at Tell Hariri, in modern Syria. The city was established early in the third millennium BCE and prospered from river trade. Discovered in 1933, the ruins have been repeatedly excavated ever since. Discoveries include the palace of Zimri-Lim, a temple of Ishtar, and huge numbers of cuneiform tablets.

NINEVEH (TELL KUYUNJIK)
This ancient site in northern Iraq is located where the Khosr River joins the Tigris River. Nineveh was settled as early as the seventh millennium BCE. It had cultural links with Sumer in the fourth millennium BCE and was chosen as capital by the Assyrian ruler Sennacherib (704–681 BCE). His grandson Ashurbanipal also built his palace here. The city was destroyed by Medes and Babylonians in 612 BCE, but continued to be settled until nearby Mosul became more important. One of the most significant of all Mesopotamian sites, Nineveh was excavated in the 19th century by A. H. Layard, George Smith, and Hormuzd Rassam, and in recent times by David Stronach.

NIPPUR (NUFFAR)
Nippur is near Najaf, about 100 miles (160 km) south of Baghdad. It was on an ancient course of the Euphrates River, the present Shatt Al-Nil waterway. Settled by 4000 BCE, Nippur became an important religious center. It was rebuilt several times, including by the Akkadian ruler Naram-Sin (r. 2254–2218 BCE). Major archeological discoveries at Nippur have included temples and stores. There is also a large ziggurat, which in the second century CE became the base of a fortress.

PERSEPOLIS (TAKHT-E JAMSHID)
This impressive site is in Iran, 45 miles (70 km) northeast of Shiraz. It is Persian, but dates from the period when Mesopotamia was part of the first Persian or Achaemenid empire. Persepolis was the ceremonial capital of Darius I (r. 522–486 BCE), who built an impressive palace there.

SUSA (SHUSH)
Susa is in southwestern Iran, in Khuzestan province. The ancient city dated from at least 4000 BCE and was the capital of the Elamite Empire. During the course of history, Susa came under Babylonian, Assyrian, Persian, and Greek rule. Darius I of Persia built a great palace here in the late sixth century BCE. The site was identified in 1851 and extensively excavated by the French.

UR (TELL AL-MUQAYYAR)
The ancient city of Ur is on the Euphrates River, near Nasiriyah in modern Iraq. It was originally near the Gulf, but over the millennia this coastline silted up so that now the site is far inland. This city is one of the world's oldest, founded some time between 5300 and 4100 BCE—a period that Mesopotamian archeologists call the Ubaid period. Ur was one of the leading Sumerian city-states and reached the height of its power under its third ruling dynasty between the years 2112 and 2004 BCE. It remained an important religious center for centuries. Frank Woolley's excavation of Ur's Royal Tombs between 1922 and 1934 produced some of the most stunning of all Mesopotamian artifacts. The site today is dominated by its impressive restored ziggurat.

URUK (WARKA)
The Euphrates, which once passed through this site, is now 8 miles (12 km) away. Warka is in Iraq, some 156 miles (250 km) southeast of Baghdad. Pottery from around 5000 BCE has been found here and by 3500 BCE this was a great religious center with many temples. It was a leading Sumerian city-state, associated with the legendary Gilgamesh and mentioned in the Bible as Erech. The site is dominated by the ziggurat of Inanna, goddess of love and war, built by Ur-Nammu around 2100 BCE.

Places to visit

BRITISH MUSEUM, LONDON, UK
www.thebritishmuseum.ac.uk
www.mesopotamia.co.uk
The British Museum's Ancient Near East collection includes monuments found by the archeologist A. H. Layard. Do not miss:
- Assyrian palace reliefs from Kalhu
- Treasures from the Royal Tombs at Ur, such as the lyre, Queen Puabi's headdress, and one of the "Rams Caught in the Thicket"
- Cuneiform tablets, including the Flood Tablet from the epic of Gilgamesh

METROPOLITAN MUSEUM OF ART, NEW YORK CITY, USA
www.metmuseum.org
The Ancient Near East galleries of the "Met" contain a wealth of Mesopotamian and Persian artifacts. Highlights include:
- Cylinder seals
- Headdress and necklace from Ur
- Statue of Gudea of Lagash
- Babylonian jewelry

MUSEE DU LOUVRE, PARIS, FRANCE
www.louvre.fr
The Louvre's department of Near East Antiquities holds many of the fine artifacts discovered by the great 19th-century archeologists. Be sure to look for::
- The stele of Hammurabi, featuring one of the world's earliest legal codes
- Assyrian monuments from Sargon II's palace at Khorsabad
- Alabaster panels from Kalhu

The Musée du Louvre, Paris

IRAQ MUSEUM, BAGHDAD, IRAQ
www.baghdadmuseum.org
This is the national collection of Iraq, currently sealed off from public exhibition following the tragic looting of precious artifacts from the museum at the start of the Iraq War in 2003. The museum's treasures may still be viewed online. The collection includes:
- The so-called Mona Lisa of Nimrud
- Lion hunt images from ancient Uruk
- Carved ivories from Nimrud

PERGAMON MUSEUM, BERLIN, GERMANY
www.smb.spk-berlin.de
Berlin's remarkable Museum of the Ancient Near East is part of the Pergamon Museum complex. It houses classic Mesopotamian discoveries brought back by the great German archeologists, and painstakingly assembled recreations. Attractions include:
- Reconstruction of Babylon's fabulous Ishtar Gate and the Processional Way
- Some of the world's earliest writing
- Assyrian palace reliefs from Nimrud

Glossary

Cylinder seal (right) and its impression (left)

AKKADIAN (1) From Akkad, the region to the north of Sumer. (2) One of a family of Semitic languages, whose northern dialect is Assyrian and southern dialect is Babylonian.

AKITU Ancient Babylon's spring festival to mark the New Year and honor the god Marduk.

ALABASTER A white, translucent stone.

ALLOY A mixture of two metals (such as tin and copper) to form one material (such as bronze).

AQUEDUCT A channel built to carry water, especially one supported by a bridge.

ARCHEOLOGY The systematic study of ancient ruins and remains.

ASSYRIAN (1) From Assyria, a region of northern Mesopotamia. (2) The ancient language spoken by Assyrians.

ASTROLOGER Someone who studies the movements of the stars and planets and believes that they affect the lives of humans.

BABYLONIAN (1) From the city-state of Babylon or the Babylonian empire. (2) The ancient language spoken by Babylonians.

BARSOM For Medes and Persians, a bundle of sticks used to connect with godly powers.

BITUMEN Naturally occurring tar, used in ancient Mesopotamia for building and crafts.

BULLA (1) The Latin word for various round objects, such as a bubble, talisman, or locket. (2) In Sumerian archeology, a clay sphere containing tokens used in record-keeping.

CARNELIAN A red quartz used in jewelry.

CHARIOT A wheeled vehicle, usually drawn by horses, used in battle, racing, or hunting.

CITY-STATE A small state or nation based upon a single city or a small group of cities.

CIVILIZATION An organized society that has made advances in government, law, justice, the arts, science, and technology.

CIVIL SERVANT A public official.

CULTURE (1) A way of life particular to a community or other social grouping. (2) The arts, literature, or music.

CUNEIFORM SCRIPT Wedge-shaped symbols, a form of writing developed by the Sumerians.

CYLINDER SEAL A small stone cylinder engraved with an image. It was rolled over soft clay to reproduce the image, which functioned as a personal seal on packages, locks, or tablets.

DEATH PIT A room adjoining the main burial chamber in the Royal Tombs of Ur, filled with the bodies of sacrificed servants and officials.

DECIMAL SYSTEM A system of counting or measurement whose units are based on 10.

DEITY A god or goddess.

DIADEM A jeweled headband or crown.

DIORITE A greenstone used for sculpture that contains the minerals felspar and hornblende.

DIVINATION Foretelling future events by looking for omens or by carrying out rituals.

DOMESTICATION The taming and breeding of wild animals by humans in order to make use of them in farming, hunting, and haulage.

DYNASTY A royal family and its period of rule.

ECLIPSE When one heavenly body passes into the shadow of another, so that its light (or its reflected light) is blocked out for a short time.

EDUBBA A school. The word literally means "house of tablets," a place where one writes words or numbers on clay tablets.

EINKORN One of the first forms of wheat to be cultivated in the Fertile Crescent.

EMMER Another early form of wheat cultivated by farmers in the Fertile Crescent.

EMPIRE A group of lands or peoples brought under the rule of a single government or king.

ENTRAILS Guts. Priests examined the entrails of animals sacrificed to the gods to tell the future.

EPIC A poetic tale of heroes and gods.

ETEMMU According to Mesopotamian mythology, birdlike spirits of the dead, who live in the underworld and feed off clay.

FERTILE CRESCENT A broad belt of land, stretching westward from Mesopotamia, which 10,000 years ago was suitable for growing crops.

FLAX A blue-flowered plant whose fiber is used to make linen, and whose seed is used to make oil.

Hittite war chariot

GENIE OR DJINN A powerful spirit in the ancient mythologies of the Middle East.

GILD To coat something with gold.

GLAZE A glossy, glasslike finish on pottery.

GRAVE GOODS Valuable or useful objects placed in a tomb, for use in the afterlife.

HELLENISTIC In the tradition of Greek culture.

HIERATIC SCRIPT A script used in Ancient Egypt from about 2700 to 700 BCE.

HITTITE (1) Relating to a people who established themselves in Anatolia, dominating large areas of western Asia from the 1600s to the 1200s. (2) The language spoken by Hittites.

Brightly painted lamassu

Artist's impression of Assyrian throne room at Nimrud (ancient Kalhu) c. 850 BCE

Mede carrying a barsom

IRRIGATION Bringing water to crops by means of channels, ditches, or pipes.

KARUM An Akkadian word for a merchant or trading colony.

KILN A high-temperature oven used for firing pottery or bricks.

KING LISTS Inscribed clay tablets recording the reigns and dynasties of the Sumerian kings.

LAMASSU A huge Assyrian stone statue of a winged bull or lion with a human head.

LAPIS LAZULI A deep blue stone from Afghanistan, valued for its use in jewelry.

LEGAL CODE A summary of the laws which apply in a country.

LOOM A framework used for weaving textiles.

LYRE A musical instrument popular in Mesopotamia, ancient Egypt, Greece, and Rome. It had a soundbox, two arms, and a yoke or crossbar supporting the strings.

MACE (1) A war club. (2) A scepter used as a symbol of authority.

Obelisk detailing tribute to Shalmaneser III (858–824 BCE)

MALACHITE A green-colored gemstone.

MASTIFF A heavy and powerful hunting dog.

MESOPOTAMIA A Greek term meaning "between rivers," used to describe the lands around the Tigris and Euphrates rivers.

MILLENNIUM A period of 1,000 years.

MINA A unit of weight in ancient Mesopotamia, roughly equal to 18 oz (500 g).

MINARET A tower in a mosque, from which Muslims are called to prayer five times a day.

MOAT A defensive water-filled ditch surrounding the walls of a castle or a city.

MUSHHUSHSHU A mythical snake-dragon, associated with the god Marduk.

MYTH A traditional tale that attempts to explain the natural world or other phenomena. It may feature imaginary beasts, gods, spirits, or heroes.

NOMAD Someone who does not lead a settled existence, but moves from place to place, seeking new pastures for grazing animals.

OBELISK A tall, four-sided pillar of stone, pointed at the top, serving as a monument.

ONAGER A wild pony of western Asia, hunted and used for haulage in Mesopotamia.

PAPYRUS Paper made from a type of reed.

PATRIARCH In the early scriptures of Jews, Christians, and Muslims, a founding father of the tribe.

PRECINCT An area that has been set aside or enclosed, often because it is regarded as sacred ground.

QUFFA A round, waterproof, wicker row boat of Mesopotamia, similar to a coracle.

RITUAL A formalized set of actions and words in which gods are worshipped or asked for help.

RHYTON A metal drinking cup in the shape of a horn.

ROD A Babylonian unit of measurement, roughly equal to 20 ft (6 m).

SCEPTER A staff or mace carried by kings as an emblem of royalty.

SCRIBE A professional writer or copier of texts, a clerk in the ancient world.

SEXAGESIMAL SYSTEM A system of counting or measurement whose units are based on 60. It is still used to count seconds, minutes, and hours, and to define the degrees of a circle.

SHADUF A bucket, skin, or other container attached to a weighted pole, and used to raise water from a river.

SHEKEL (1) A unit of weight in Ancient Babylon, equal to one-sixtieth of a mina—about 8.3 g (¼ oz). (2) Silver currency of this weight.

SHRINE A sacred place dedicated to or associated with a god, spirit, or holy object.

SLING SHOT A small stone hurled from a whirling string—a primitive but deadly weapon.

SMELT To separate metal from its ore by melting it.

SPHINX A mythical creature with the body of a lion and the head of a human.

Ivory carving of a sphinx, c. 750 BCE

SPINDLE A weighted, twirling rod used to spin fiber from yarn.

STELE An upright slab or pillar of stone, bearing an inscription or image.

STYLUS A pointed instrument used to write characters on a soft surface such as wax or clay. In Mesopotamia, a stylus was generally made of cut reed.

SUMERIAN (1) From Sumer, the southernmost region of Mesopotamia. (2) The language spoken in Sumer.

TABLET A small slab of clay, used for writing cuneiform script with a reed stylus.

TELL A mound containing the remains of different periods of settlement, which has slowly built up over the ages.

TEXTILE Any fabric created by weaving.

TRIBUTE Valuable goods paid by one king to another as a recognition of the other's superior status as overlord.

ZIGGURAT A multistorey temple platform or mound, in the form of a stepped pyramid, with a shrine to a god on the top. Most ziggurats were first built in the late third millennium BCE.

Index

Acknowledgments

The publisher would like to thank the following: Claire Bowers, David Eckold–JAlbum, Sunita Gahir, Joanne Little, Susan St. Louis, Steve Setford, and Bulent Yusef for the clip art; David Ball, Neville Graham, Rose Horridge, Joanne Little, and Susan Nicholson for the wall chart; Andy Hilliard, Ben Hung, and Ronaldo Julien for DTP support; and Lynn Bresler for proofreading and the index.

Picture Credits:
The publisher would like to thank the following for their kind permission to reproduce their photographs:

Key: a-above; b-bottom; bl-bottom left; br-bottom right; c-center; cl-center left; cr-center right; crb-center right below; l-left; r-right; t-top; tl-top left; tr-top right. ftr-far top right; bc-below

center; crb-center right below; fclb-far center left below; fcrb-far center right below; fcla-far center left above.

akg-images: 9c, 22l, 55cla; Gérard Degeorge 61tl; Erich Lessing 15br, 16c, 17tl, 19tr, 23l, 24cr, 26br, 27tl, 27bl, 30bl, 36tl, 39cr, 41br, 42-43, 48l, 58tr, 66b, 71cr; **Alamy Images:** Arcaid 33cr; Tor Eigeland 51br; Vario Images GmbH & Co.KG 63tc; **Ancient Art & Architecture Collection:** 42tl; G. T. Garvey 56-57c; Prisma 57tr; **The Art Archive:** Archaeological Museum Bagdad / Dagli Orti 59l; British Museum/Dagli Orti 16t; Christies/ Eileen Tweedy 14cr; Musée du Louvre Paris / Dagli Orti 9br, 11br, 13t, 19cr, 24cl, 25tl, 55crb; Dagli Orti 57cr; **Zainab Bahrani:** 63c; **Joanne Farchakh Bajjaly:** 7cl; **Bildarchiv Preußischer Kulturbesitz, Berlin:** Dist RMN/Klaus Göken 26bl;

Vorderasiatisches Museum 5, 28-29tl, 50br, 52tl, 54-55t; The **Bridgeman Art Library:** 15t, 25tc, 38tl, 52bl, 64b, 68bl; Ashmolean Museum, Oxford 21br, 37br, 42cl; Bibliothèque des Arts Decoratifs, Paris 47bc; Bibliothèque Nationale, Paris 47c, 61bl; British Museum, London 46br, 48cr, 49tr, 67bl; Iraq Museum, Baghdad 17cl; Kunsthistorisches Museum, Vienna, Austria 25tr; Louvre, Paris, France/ Giraudon 10bl; **British Library:** 60cl; 61tr; **The Trustees of the British Museum:** 7r, 12b, 14cl, 21tr, 21cl, 21bl, 28bl, 29tc, 29r, 30bc, 31cr, 32l, 33tr, 34cl, 34-35, 36tr, 36-37c, 43br, 44-45b, 50bl, 51t, 51bc, 53bl, 54cl, 56l, 59cr, 60tr, 62tl, 66tl, 69l, 71tl, 71bl; Corbis: 68b; The Art Archive 46-47br; Bettmann 21tl, 62bl, 67br; David Butow 7tl; EPA 45tr; David Lees 6br; Araldo de Luca 58tl; Gianni Dagli Orti 65t; © Spc Katherine M Roth/HO/epa 43tr; Werner Forman 45tl; Nik Wheeler 8cr, 19tl, 31br, 41tl, 48b; Roger Wood 59br; Michael S.Yamashita 8bl, 24-25b; **DK Images:** 39tr; British

Museum, London 7bl, 8-9t, 10-11, 12cl, 20-21c, 27br, 28-29bc, 30-31c, 39cl, 42bl; Judith Miller 6bl; **Getty Images:** 63tr; **Michael Holford:** 12cr, 31tr, 32-33, 40tl, 40bl, 44tr; **Images and Stories:** 55br; **Bill Lyons:** 46cl; **Mary Evans Picture Library:** 13b, 46bl; **National Gallery, London:** 53br; **Peter Langer/Associated Media Group:** 17bc, 24tl; Réunion des Musées Nationaux Agence Photographique: J. G. Berizzi 15bl; Gérard Blot 12t; Hervé Lewandowski 4cr, 11tr, 26t, 35cr, 57br; Michel Urtado 23br; **Photo Scala, Florence:** 10tl, 23cr; The Iraq Museum, Baghdad 35bc, 63br; **TopFoto.co.uk:** 6t, 67t; British Museum/HIP 20tr; **University of Pennsylvania Museum:** 16b, 23tr.

Wall chart:
akg images/Erich Lessing: tl, fclb; **Ancient Art and Architecture Collection:** fcrb; **Bildarchiv Preußischer Kulturbesitz/ Vorderasiatisches Museum:** bc; **Bridgeman Art Library/British**

Museum: crb; **Réunion des Musées Nationaux Agence Photographique/** Hervé Lewandowski: br; Photo Scala, Florence: ftr, fcla.

Jacket:
Front: **Alamy Images:** Images & Stories ftl; **The Bridgeman Art Library:** National Museum, Aleppo, Syria/ Giraudon b; **The Trustees of the British Museum:** tca; **Corbis:** Michael S. Yamashita tr; **DK Images:** The Trustees of the British Museum tc. *Back:* **Ancient Art & Architecture Collection:** clb; **The Art Archive:** Musee du Louvre, Paris/Dagli Orti bl; **The Bridgeman Art Library:** Iraq Museum, Baghdad br; **The Trustees of the British Museum:** c, cb, crb; **Corbis:** Edifice tl.

All other images © Dorling Kindersley

For further information see:
www.dkimages.com